AI and the Future of Leadership

AI and the Future of Leadership explores the profound implications of artificial intelligence for leadership theory and practice. As Artificial Intelligence (AI) technologies become increasingly embedded in organisational life, this book interrogates the readiness of current leadership models to adapt to an era of automation, algorithms and accelerated change. Blending critical insight with real-world relevance, the book examines the promises and perils of AI in the workplace – from wellbeing and resistance to innovation and control. It highlights the limits of conventional leadership paradigms and proposes a new framework for 'hybrid intelligence leadership' suited to the complexities of human–machine collaboration. Designed to stimulate debate and advance understanding, this book offers fresh perspectives for scholars and practitioners navigating the fast-evolving AI landscape. It equips readers to think strategically and ethically about leadership in organisations that are increasingly shaped by intelligent systems. It will appeal to academics, researchers, educators and advanced students in leadership, management and organisational studies. It will also be of interest to professionals and policymakers seeking to understand how leadership must evolve to meet the demands of the AI age.

Adrian Jarvis is Senior Lecturer in Education in the Department of Education in the School of Business, Education and Law at the University of Huddersfield, UK.

Routledge Focus on Business and Management

The fields of business and management have grown exponentially as areas of research and education. This growth presents challenges for readers trying to keep up with the latest important insights. *Routledge Focus on Business and Management* presents small books on big topics and how they intersect with the world of business research.

Individually, each title in the series provides coverage of a key academic topic, whilst collectively, the series forms a comprehensive collection across the business disciplines.

Sustainable Organizational Change
The Social Change Model for Systems
Joshua D. Burton and Barbara Carter

Entrepreneurship Education and Student Empowerment
Innovation in the EU
Chiara Bartoli and Federica Brunetta

Critical Thinking in Public Policy and Management
Michael Macaulay

Digital Social Entrepreneurship
Implications for People, Planet and Profit
Edited by Veronica Scuotto, Norris Krueger and Manlio Del Giudice

AI and the Future of Leadership
Opportunities and Threats for Hybrid Organisations
Adrian Jarvis

For more information about this series, please visit: www.routledge.com/Routledge-Focus-on-Business-and-Management/book-series/FBM

AI and the Future of Leadership

Opportunities and Threats for Hybrid Organisations

Adrian Jarvis

Routledge
Taylor & Francis Group
NEW YORK AND LONDON

First published 2026
by Routledge
605 Third Avenue, New York, NY 10158

and by Routledge
4 Park Square, Milton Park, Abingdon, Oxon, OX14 4RN

Routledge is an imprint of the Taylor & Francis Group, an informa business

ISBN: 978-1-041-12584-6 (hbk)
ISBN: 978-1-041-12585-3 (pbk)
ISBN: 978-1-003-66553-3 (ebk)

DOI: 10.4324/9781003665533

Typeset in Times New Roman
by KnowledgeWorks Global Ltd.

Dedicated to my wife, Karen

Contents

Acknowledgements

This book would not exist without the excellent editing of Brianna Ascher and Jessica Rech. The case studies have been developed with the help of Abd-Al Basit, Stella Bowdell, Ian Crum, Katey Curtis, Guy Feld, Alastair Morris, Richard Paxman and Stuart Pugh. Consultancy and peer review have been provided by Dr Donnie Adams, Dr Emma Arakas, Professor Richard Bailey, Dr George Bargianis, Dr Dorrie Chao and Dr Michael Hall. More generally, the leadership ideas that are the spine of the argument have emerged over time from research that I have undertaken with Ra'ed Ali Mohammad Al-khamaiseh, Dr Suria Angit, Dr Shamsiah Banu, Abu Rusho Hussain, Dr Simranjeet Kaur Judge, Dr Pradip Kumar Mishra, Dr Marc Turu Purcel and Anika Rahman. It need hardly be said that I am entirely at fault for any inaccuracies or absurdities contained herein.

1 Introduction

Living with AI

1.1 Perspectives on Artificial Intelligence

Artificial Intelligence (AI) has arrived (Mayer et al., 2025). Consisting of computer systems that can engage in machine learning, produce outputs and manage processes, AI is already demonstrating bewildering capabilities and will continue to evolve in ways that are difficult to forecast. Like any nascent technology, it is currently more present in some countries than others (Khan et al., 2024), but it represents the future for everyone. It will be a part of work and leisure. It will change thought patterns and social relationships. It will influence the way that society and organisations are constituted and led.

Yet, AI is not a new idea. Even in Ancient Greece, stories showcased a fascination with sentient artificial beings (Haynes, 2023). In arguably the most famous, Pygmalion, a sculptor, creates a statue of a woman, which he names Galatea, who is so beautiful that he prays for her to be made real. His wish is duly granted by the goddess Aphrodite. The flesh Galatea appears fully equipped with cognitive functions and a personality. A different slant is offered by Mary Shelley's 1818 novel *Frankenstein* (Shelley, 2003). The titular character, a scientist, attempts to build a living human from stolen body parts that he brings together and re-animates through a process about which he remains deliberately coy. The result is not the *ubermensch* that he envisaged, but an ugly 'creature' that becomes a ruthless killer and, ultimately, Frankenstein's nemesis. The story has become so ingrained in world culture that the prefix 'Franken-' is routinely applied to any scientific breakthrough that causes alarm or unease (Ruston & Smith, 2019). AI has been called 'Frankentech' by some (Skidelsky, 2023).

Rarely remarked upon is how Frankenstein's creature operates, both physically and mentally. None of his parts, apparently, has a connection back to the person who supplied it. This is of little consequence for limbs and internal organs, which perform in exactly the same way as they always have, but the creature's brain is more problematic. It does not carry with it

DOI: 10.4324/9781003665533-1

the consciousness of whichever individual contributed it. It seems to have been acquired as a piece of dead matter. The creature thus enjoys no continuity with the person, or people, that he once was but is 'born' an adult with a mind that is a child-like *tabula rasa*, empty of content and in need of being 'programmed.' Indeed, the central thrust of the novel is the creature learning about the world and his place within it.

The creature's mind is a construct. It owes nothing to nature. Galatea's consciousness is a divine gift, but the creature's exists because Frankenstein brings it into being. It is an AI and, as much as Shelley cannot be said to have invented the concept to which we now apply that abbreviation, or even to have necessarily predicted it, she can be credited with supplying a potent metaphor for it (one, indeed, that is evoked in most writings on the subject). A common interpretation is to see her work as a warning about the dangers of technology; in response to various unpleasant stimuli, the creature abandons his initial desire to be 'benevolent' and turns his anger against those he regards as his persecutors. As will be seen, *Frankenstein* the novel was certainly prescient in its anticipation of debates around such dangers.

In a literal sense, nothing approximating to Frankenstein's creature has ever been created. A modern version – although perhaps Galatea is the more apt original – might be Lili Ziren, an actor who has a main role in the Chinese television series, *I Am Nobody*. Although she interacts with her co-stars and the environments in which the story takes place, she is not a real person. She is a programme created by the corporation Alibaba using AI. She is not based on any specific individual. Analogously to Frankenstein's creature, several human templates were used to bring her to life. She is astonishingly convincing. Her hair falls around her face with a realistic randomness, she sweats and twitches, her skin has pores and wrinkles. Many watching her in action have claimed that it is impossible to tell that she is not every bit as human as anyone else on the screen.

Lili is not the only non-existent person to be currently amassing fame in some part of the media. AI-generated influencers on Tik Tok and Instagram are increasingly common (Looi & Kahlor, 2024): they gather thousands of followers with whom they interact fluently – and lucratively. In a more banal way, every time an online customer has a text 'chat' with a personal guide, the helpful advice that they receive is likely bestowed by an AI 'bot' (Lin et al., 2024).

While these examples could be taken to represent the possibilities and dangers of AI, they are more intriguing for what they suggest about the relative positioning of AI and human beings. Hitherto, information technology has been a useful tool with which to carry out a wide range of tasks, from office work to design, to artistic endeavours and so on. It has become increasingly sophisticated over time, but it remains a method by which people can do their jobs more easily: the jobs still have to be done by people. Even in those areas in which information technology operates with minimal interference, it has to be programmed in advance. It has no power to make decisions on its own behalf and, in some occupations, may even be, on balance, disadvantageous (Perez et al., 2022).

If AI achieves anything approaching the potential that many authors claim it will (Ziesche, 2025), it will demand from people a whole new mindset. They will not use AI, they will work alongside it (Zirar et al., 2023). In other words, they will not be in a relationship *to* AI but in a relationship *with* it. AI will be, in a very real sense, at least a colleague and perhaps a friend and confidant. Perhaps again, it will be a rival. It will certainly be capable of working independently and taking over many of the jobs currently done by human beings. Organisations will no longer be collections of people in command of the tools they use, including information technology, but combinations of people and AI, each with their own specific areas of responsibility; they will be human–AI hybrid organisations (Fabri et al., 2023).

Such social and technological developments will result in any number of the opportunities and threats that this book explores. Above all, they will demand a new style of leadership. Old ideas about leadership as an influence relationship centred on motivating followers to reach given goals will not be adequate to the challenges of running the organisations of the future. New approaches will be required: what those might be is the main question that this book seeks to answer. Given the novelty of the topic and the speculative nature of much of the thinking around it, the book's chief methodology is theoretical discussion, reinforced with examples and case studies of (in all but one instance) small- to medium-size enterprises (SMEs) chosen for their suitability to illustrate key arguments and concepts. Data about the case study organisations have been gathered through interviews, content analyses of documents and consultancy. The case study organisations being modest in scale underlines the potential penetration of AI into every business function. This book, therefore, is a perspective piece that addresses an issue of contemporary concern from a largely conceptual standpoint (Narula, 2024).

The argument begins by looking at definitions of intelligence and Artificial Intelligence. These are problematised in Chapter 2, which considers the nature of AI with an emphasis on how it might operate with human beings. In Chapter 3, the major threats and opportunities of AI are considered. Those that will have a bearing on leadership are foregrounded. The specific case of AI resistance occupies Chapter 4, since it is among the most salient of issues for leaders moving forward. Following this, leadership itself is considered. The purpose of this chapter, Chapter 5, is to place leadership into a theoretical context, thus setting up the next stage of the argument. This is engaged with in the sixth chapter which looks at the leadership challenges of AI: the point is to make use of the theoretical background already explored to go deeper than to simply look at leadership activities. To some extent, these form the substance of Chapter 7, which aims to outline a practice for leaders in an age informed, if not dominated, by AI. A criterion for success is suggested. An overall approach is proposed in the concluding eighth chapter.

1.2 The Difficulties of Defining 'Artificial Intelligence'

To avoid uncritically accepting the many prophecies about AI propounded in both the media and the academic literature (Gruetzemacher & Whittlestone, 2022), it is necessary at the beginning to be clear about what is meant by 'artificial intelligence'. This is far from simple because there is as yet not even a consensus about what is meant by 'intelligence' (Toon, 2024).

Semantically, 'intelligence' belongs to a whole field of related terms, including 'consciousness,' 'self-consciousness' and 'mind' which remain difficult to either define or explain, but which have a bearing on any discussion about AI. To suggest that intelligence is an aspect of a person's mental world is highly reductive, as is the common lay notion of it as 'especially powerful mental capabilities'. More specifically, intelligence has often been subcategorised as 'crystallised' and 'fluid' (Coane et al., 2023). The former refers, essentially, to knowledge gained through experience, the latter an ability to solve problems without reference to crystallised knowledge. Intelligence is thus both receptive and active; it can be defined as an awareness of the world and a capacity to act on that awareness.

Like many concepts in psychology, though, this is contested. A good question would be whether it is ever possible to face a situation in an entirely context-free manner; crystallised intelligence is likely to be called upon in some form irrespective of the novelty of the situation in which an actor finds themselves. With this in mind, Sternberg (1999) posited the notion of 'general intelligence' or expertise. This is an accumulation of crystallised knowledge that can be be applied to problem-solving situations. Sternberg divided general intelligence into three elements, the analytic – broadly, academic intelligence – the creative – the ability to initiate - and the practical – which is action-orientated knowledge achieved through personal experience (Sternberg, 1985).

As brief as this discussion might be, it illustrates the essential point that any concept or definition of 'artificial intelligence' is elusive. Given the vagueness of intelligence as a phenomenon, statements to the effect that AI is a computer programme that mimics human intelligence is rendered immediately inadequate (Sheikh et al., 2023). Moreover, Moravec's Paradox (Arora, 2023) adds further distance between the human and the artificial. This points out that tasks which computers carry out easily are very difficult for human beings – but the reverse is also true. So, computers can instantly solve mathematical problems that would stump the most powerful human minds, but everyday activities such as frying an egg or ironing clothes require tacit calculative power beyond that of any machine yet devised. Lili Ziren might interact with real actors, but she is not physically present when they are giving their performances. Stand-ins are used over which she is placed later. She is, basically, an animation added in post-production. A physical robot so lifelike that observers cannot tell the difference between it and a genuine person lies a long way in the future.

Nonetheless, it would be complacent to ignore the pace of change in AI, especially in its ever-greater degree of autonomy. AI as intelligence has largely been analytic up to now, but it is annexing the territory of all three of Sternberg's (1985) elements at a rate that renders most commentary on the matter out of date almost as soon as it is written. AI is increasingly able to operate remote from human control. Many authors argue that it is on its way to becoming its own type of 'general intelligence' (McLean et al., 2023), which is the condition – theoretical at the time of writing – of AI being indistinguishable from human intelligence: an AGI (artificial general intelligence) would learn, reason and apply knowledge across a wide range of scenarios in exactly the same way that human beings do. Beyond that, Kurzweil (2006) predicts a future 'singularity' when AI would bring about a historic watershed by finally outperforming human beings in every cognitive function and having no further use for them (Hoffmann, 2023). By then, it is said, AI – or 'strong AI' – would have achieved self-consciousness, if, as some fear, it has not done so already (Hildt, 2019). It can only be hoped that it proves to be a loving Galatea and not a vengeful Frankenstein's creature.

Such prognostications have more than a hint of science fiction about them, but what can be said for certain is that AI will have a significant impact on work and the running of organisations. That process is already well underway. Healthcare, administration and the military are some areas being enriched or destroyed by AI – depending on one's perspective (Sharma & Biros, 2021). Where AI, for example, improves the accuracy of medical diagnoses, it can be described as wholly beneficial, but that is not to ignore the controversies that are raging in such industries as education, where AI's potential for good or bad remains undecided (Luckin, 2025). Either way, what AI is now, and what it will likely become, should be uppermost in the minds of organisational leaders in all sectors of activity.

References

Arora, A. (2023). Moravec's paradox and the fear of job automation in health care. *The Lancet*, 402(10397), 180–181.

Coane, J. H., Cipollini, J., Barrett, T. E., Kavaler, J. & Umanath, S. (2023). Lay definitions of intelligence, knowledge and memory: Inter- and independence of constructs. *Journal of Intelligence*, 11(5), 84.

Fabri, L., Hackel, B., Oberlander, A. M., Ring, M. & Stohr, A. (2023). Disentangling human-AI hybrids. *Business Information Systems Engineering*, 65(6), 623–641.

Gruetzemacher, R. & Whittlestone, J. (2022). The transformative potential of artificial intelligence. *Futures*, 135, 102884.

Haynes, M. (2023). The skin of a statue: Rethinking Ovid's pygmalion. *Sculpture Journal*, 32(2), 175–191.

Hildt, E. (2019). Artificial intelligence: Does consciousness matter? *Frontiers in Psychology*, 10(2019), 1535.

Hoffmann, C. H. (2023). A philosophical view on singularity and strong AI. *AI & Society*, 38(4), 1697–1714.

Khan, M. S., Umer, H. & Faruge, F. (2024). Artificial intelligence for low income countries. *Humanities and Social Science Communications*, 11, 1422.

Kurzweil, R. (2006). *The Singularity Is Near*. Duckworth.

Lin, X., Wang, X., Shao, B. & Taylor, J. (2024). How chatbots augment human intelligence in customer services: A mixed methods study. *Journal of Management Information Systems*, 41(4), 1016–1041.

Looi, J. & Kahlor, L. A. (2024). Artificial intelligence in influencer marketing: A mixed method comparison of human and virtual influencers on Instagram. *Journal of Interactive Advertising*, 24(2), 107–126.

Luckin, R. (2025). Nurturing human intelligence in the age of AI: Rethinking education for the future. *Development and Learning in Organisations: An International Journal*, 39(1), 1–4.

Mayer, H., Yee, L., Choi, M. & Robert's, R. (2025). *Superagency in the Workplace: Empowering People to Unlock AI's Full Potential*. McKinsey & Company.

McLean, S., Read, G. J. M., Thompson, J., Baber, C., Stanton, N. A. & Salmon, P. M. (2023). The risks associated with Artificial General Intelligence: A systematic review. *Journal of Experimental & Theoretical Artificial Intelligence*, 35(5), 649–663.

Narula, R. (2024). On writing a perspectives article – what they are, what they are not (and what they should be). *Journal of International Business Policy*, 7, 253–259.

Perez, H., Neubauer, N., Marshall, S., Philip, S., Miguel-Cruz, A. & Lui, L. (2022). Barriers and benefits of information communication technologies used by health care aides. *Applied Clinical Informatics*, 13(1), 270–286.

Ruston, S. & Smith, R. (2019). Introduction. *Nineteenth-Century Contexts*, 41(3), 237–242.

Sharma, M. & Biros, D. (2021). AI and its implications for organisations. In Z. W. Y. Lee, T. K. H. Chan & C. M. K. Cheung (Eds), *Information Technology in Organisations and Societies: Multidisciplinary Perspectives from AI to Technostress* (pp. 1–24). Emerald Publishing Ltd.

Sheikh, H., Prins, C. & Schrijvers, E. (2023). Artificial intelligence: Definition and background. In H. Sheikh, C. Prins & E. Shrijvers (Eds.), *Mission AI*. Springer.

Shelley, M. (2003). *Frankenstein*. Penguin Books.

Skidelsky, R. (2023). Frankentech. *Project Syndicate*, https://www.project-syndicate.org/commentary/artificial-intelligence-tech-leaders-cannot-be-trusted-by-robert-skidelsky-2023-04 [accessed May 25th 2025].

Sternberg, R. J. (1985). Implicit theories of intelligence, creativity and wisdom. *Journal of Personality and Social Psychology*, 49, 607–627.

Sternberg, R. J. (1999). Intelligence as developing expertise. *Contemporary Educational Psychology*, 24, 359–375.

Toon, N. (2024). *How AI Thinks*. Random House.

Ziesche, S. (2025). An AI may establish a religion. In S. Ziesche & R. V. Yampolskiy (Eds.), *Considerations on the AI Endgame: Ethics, Risks and Computational Frameworks*. CRC Press.

Zirar, A., Ali, S. I. & Islam, N. (2023). Worker and workplace artificial intelligence (AI) coexistence: Emerging themes and research agenda. *Technovation*, 124(1), 102747.

2 What Is AI and Where Is It Going?

2.1 The Imitation Game

There are several Artificial Intelligence (AI) technologies and algorithms but the one with which lay people will have greatest familiarity is the Transformer. This is a type of chatbot that leverages 'large language models' (LLM). Among the most prominent transformers at present is ChatGPT from the company OpenAI. LLMs are programmes that generate text by predicting the next words in sentences or paragraphs, which they can do having undergone 'deep learning' – a development of the more established machine learning (Raiaan et al., 2024). Once 'trained', LLMs are equipped to notice patterns and links among and between words and phrases in order to produce outputs that are mostly, but not necessarily, written. This is referred to as natural language processing (NLP) (Gruetzemacher, 2022). Any type of text can be generated in this way – often in moments – from essays to reports to obituaries. LLMs can also translate, summarise and provide the words for online customer service chatbots.

Deep learning uses massive data sets consisting of texts that, in some way, need to be 'completed'. Some LLMs are presented with extracts that have had words masked out, the requirement being to use prediction and logic to fill in what is missing. Others use causal modelling to predict the next words in sentences. It all sounds highly automated, but human interventions are not completely absent. As Murgia (2024) has revealed, much of the data for deep learning are sorted and rated by workers in offices, a high proportion of which are based in developing countries. In theory, this stage will eventually be made obsolete by AI becoming its own teacher.

The most remarkable feature of LLMs is their capacity to respond to questions and instructions in a human-like way. ChatGPT works by the user inputting a request – for example, 'write a sonnet about leadership' – only for the answer to appear as if by magic.

Here is a sonnet about leadership generated by ChatGPT:

A leader stands with steady, steadfast grace,
Not swayed by winds or fleeting tides of fame.

DOI: 10.4324/9781003665533-2

With vision clear, they guide through time and space,
And lift the hearts of those who call their name.

Their strength is not in force or sharp command,
But in the trust they earn and wisdom shared.
They lead with empathy, a steady hand,
And in their courage, all the crowd is paired.

Through darkest nights, they light the path ahead,
With hope as bright as stars in skies of grey.
Their purpose strong, their spirit never dead,
A beacon burning in the vast array.

For true leadership is not just to lead,
But to inspire others to take the seed.

Since this has come from a machine, it is certainly artificial, but whether it qualifies as evidence of intelligence is open to debate. No-one could doubt that it takes intelligence to build the programme that wrote it, but that does not mean that the programme itself is intelligent. How far AI is genuinely intelligent is still a matter of controversy. It is far from clear how intelligence would be manifest if it were. Are LLMs, therefore, intelligent in the same way that human beings are intelligent (Legg & Hutter, 2007)?

ChatGPT's outputs might suggest 'yes', but in reaching that conclusion, confirmation bias is a danger (Ha & Kim, 2024). It could be argued that people see intelligence in the products of LLMs because they want to. An analogy might be the owners of pets who claim to spot signs of love in their animals. There is every reason for them to do so. The animals may seem happy when their owners arrive back after a trip away; they may sleep close to their owners; they may even bring their owners unwanted tributes in the form of their latest kills. As much as these actions imply the presence of human-like emotions, there is no scientific evidence that animals feel love, or that, even if they did, they would bestow it upon members of a species other than their own. Pet owners are not seeing genuine love: they are interpreting external signs and behaviours as love (Haddy et al., 2023). It is possible that users of LLMs are doing something similar: seeing a human-like output as proof of a human-like intelligence. This is the theme of Searle's Chinese Room thought experiment (Searle, 1999), which is premised on the notion that actions could suggest intelligence where no such thing exists if an actor follows a set of rules unthinkingly. The above sonnet – irrespective of its literary merit – could have been written by a human hand. It was not. It is the outcome of a transformer using a self-attention mechanism that assesses the relative importance of words within a sentence to create complex patterns and relationships between them.

The classic test for machine intelligence was devised by the English scientist Alan Turing in 1950 in the guise of another thought experiment (Turing, 1950).

Turing argued that, if an interrogator were to pose questions to two unknown responders, one human and one a machine, but could not tell which answer came from which responder, then that would be evidence that the machine had an intelligence of its own distinct from that of its human creators.

Turing's test continues to be referenced but it is not without its drawbacks. Turing was working when computing was at a primitive stage of development. The internet did not exist and computers could do little more than carry out calculations that were relatively impressive but well within the compass of any smartphone today. Turing's 'imitation game' imagined technology that could only be found in science fiction stories at the time (Mitchell, 2024). Computing power has since caught up with Turing's forecasts. As long ago as the 1980s, 'expert system' AI architecture routinely made decisions that could be called autonomous (Giacaglia, 2021). Constrained by strict rules and with a limited menu of outcomes, expert systems operated on the 'if, then' principle: if certain conditions pertained, then a specific action would be triggered. This was useful in industries that relied on responding to fast-moving events. In finance, expert systems were programmed to react to the price of a share dropping below a certain level with an automatic 'sell' command. The domino effect that could result was one cause of the 1987 Stock Market crash (Carlson, 2006).

Expert systems may or may not have met the basic definition of intelligence, but whether they would have passed the Turing Test is a moot point. LLM-based architectures are vastly more complex, but the same can be said of them (Borg, 2025). Perhaps this is not a problem. Owners of pets might plausibly claim that, even if they are suffering from confirmation bias, the fact is immaterial. They still have a relationship with their animals and what they receive for it might not be love but it seems to be. Whatever it is, it gives the owners the feeling of being loved. AI is perhaps no different; as long as it seems human, it does not matter that it is not.

This discussion might take its cues from the mundane, but it is nonetheless to enter the realm of the philosophical. As far back as 1968, Arthur C. Clarke used the fictional computer HAL to speculate about whether conversations around the ability of machines to think are more the province of the metaphysician than the technologist (Clarke, 1968). A feature that contributes to the impression of human-like intelligence in AI is its lack of explainability (Saranya & Subhashini, 2023). Expert systems follow readily comprehensible steps; how AI reaches its conclusions is not so clear and framing the process in everyday language is even more difficult. This discussion will be revisited in a later chapter, but here it is a reminder of the complexities involved when dealing with intelligence in any of its manifestations. Using the Chinese Room as the standard, it is only external behaviours that indicate the presence of emotion in pets, or, indeed, intelligence in human beings, so there is ample reason to believe that machines, too, are not only intelligent, but conscious. Some authors believe that this is the case and that Kurzweil's singularity has already passed (Poole, 2025).

Such musings are of scant relevance here. They do, however, suggest a more fruitful direction, which is to propose that intelligence does not have to be of the same nature in every circumstance. This is not to repeat Sternberg's (1985) types of intelligence, or to mention the emotional intelligence identified by Salovey & Mayer (1990), but to question whether it is strictly necessary for the most rigorous definitions of intelligence to be met by AI. Intelligence is, after all, a spectrum (Iqbal, 2024). At one end, is will or consciousness. At the other, the unthinking obeying of simple instructions. Human intelligence is at the conscious end, but AI only has to be 'human-like' which need not imply that it, too, is in that same place.

2.2 The Purpose of Intelligence

Turing's 'imitation game' tests for intelligence but could arguably be passed only by an entity that possessed full consciousness (Goncalves, 2023). Another contested and controversial term, 'consciousness' elicits few areas of agreement other than that it includes self-awareness and a capacity for meta-cognition that makes of it something greater than simply a store of knowledge and a skill at problem-solving. Despite some of the hysterical pronouncements in recent press articles, nothing indicates that AI possesses consciousness, or ever will (Bojic et al., 2024). When the imitation game has been run for real, machines have scored badly (Goncalves, 2023). The Chinese Room, then, might be a more useful model since the standard it sets is less existential and more behavioural. In effect, it changes the question in relation to AI from 'what is intelligence' to 'what is intelligence for' – to what, in brief, is the purpose of intelligence?

For human intelligence, the answer is that it is a superbly refined survival strategy (Toon, 2024). Our earliest ancestors would have been peculiarly vulnerable to the large predators that were their chief threat. They were weaker, slower and had less highly attuned senses. They were also not particularly adept at climbing trees and could not remain for long under water – not that water afforded much protection. All animals possess forms of intelligence but the development of an unusually powerful one that learned, generalised from learning and, crucially, imagined non-existent, but possible, alternative scenarios, would have been to acquire a formidable advantage in the arms race of natural selection.

Sociality would have emerged in parallel (Pinker, 2010), bringing into being the language that is at the heart of ChatGPT and its competitors, as well as this book's chief concern, leadership. Much has been written about the origins of leadership, but the fact that numerous species demonstrate it, places it as a primal quality (Van Vugt, 2006). If fighting off sabre-toothed cats is a priority, a group has a higher chance of success than an individual. The chance is higher still if the group has unity and purpose, thus foregrounding communication and organisation as group survival characteristics. Language and leadership are the two advances that turned human herds into human societies. Neither would be possible, of course, without intelligence.

The ways in which human intelligence operates are not fully understood, but the above sketch hints at some of the complexities involved. Human intelligence is not, to start with, unitary. So far, 'intelligence' has largely been used as a synonym for 'rationality', but emotional intelligence and, underlying that, emotions themselves are not to be ignored (Van Kleef & Cote, 2022). Both are central to group cohesion and leadership, as well as the detection and countering of threats (Lerner et al., 2025).

Just as significantly for this discussion is the fact that human intelligence is not encyclopaedic, but strategic and connective (Korteling et al., 2021). Memory is not a comprehensive record of every experience that a person has ever had, but an accessible digest of the experiences most needed for making sense of the world and, thus, surviving in it. Those experiences will have been gained through interactions with physical reality. Similarly, human intelligence links information together in ways that are not always obvious; if a specific scent, for example, accompanied a key moment from childhood, that moment will forever after be evoked by the scent (Walsh, 2020).

All of this means that human intelligence is alive to context and can ascribe meanings – and symbolism – to a wide range of phenomena (Jarrahi et al., 2022). The phrase, 'if only the reds did better', would not be universally comprehensible even to humans but it would make perfect sense to someone who understood that 'the reds' denotes a football team and that their need to do better implies that they have not recently been winning games. Moreover, the phrase is in the conditional sense, so is describing not actuality, but a desired alternative to actuality.

This should not be taken as an unalloyed endorsement of human intelligence at the expense of AI. Human intelligence is limited, Moravec's paradox notwithstanding. It is true that society is more sophisticated than it was for our distant ancestors and we have overlaid upon our thinking a veneer of the abstract and academic, but we still give much of our attention to a core of activities related to survival, such as procuring food, attending to our biological functions and finding a mate. The promise of AI – the reason it has been called probably the most influential invention of all time (Losey, 2024) – is that it will serve to augment and expand the ultimately rather heavily circumscribed quality that is human intelligence, introducing to it levels of cognition that cannot be reached by finite organic brains. This is the so-called 'extended mind hypothesis' which argues that the body and the surrounding environment are involved in cognitive processes; the more that external tools – such as AI – become integrated into cognitive processes the more they cease to be crutches and become essential elements in cognitive systems and so something more like a prosthesis (Bailey et al., 2025). In answer to the question from the start of this section, that is the purpose of AI.

Unfortunately, AI does not, as yet, think like a human being. When predicting the next word in a sentence, an LLM will not make its choice based on context, nuance or strategy; it will merely consider every possible option and select the one that fits best (Blank, 2023). Not only is this far less efficient than human thought, but it can also lead to 'hallucinations' (Youssef et al., 2023). These are inaccuracies that arise from NLP. As LLMs have grown in sophistication, hallucinations have become less common but they are still an issue. Examples of hallucinations can be found in the field that has caused much debate around uses of AI: education.

It is possible to ask ChatGPT to produce a fully referenced academic essay, perhaps one on AI and the future of leadership. It will do so with improbable rapidity, but a closer look at the reference list might reveal many entries that are fictional. The AI, not knowing any better, will have treated references as a stylistic feature and included them without any understanding of their purpose. Even references that are accurate will not be to papers that the chatbot has read; the significance of the references will not have been a criterion for their inclusion. The AI does not appreciate what the references add to the argument. It knows only that a particular author is associated with a particular word, which makes the reference the most suitable in context (Mugaanyi et al., 2024). In this sense, AI can sometimes be remarkably unintelligent, exhibiting nothing more than the outwards signs of intelligence – like an inhabitant of Searle's Chinese Room. The above sonnet betrays its machine origins in being only a good example of literary form: not only is it thematically banal, but the metaphors, allusions and subtexts that imbue human-created poetry are absent.

For AI to augment and expand human intelligence, the two varieties will need to be in sync with one another. New AIs that – as of this writing – are at the early stage of development, could well bring about that eventuality.

2.3 Titans: Towards Hybrid Intelligence

The 'GPT' in ChatGPT stands for 'generative pre-trained transformer'. The sonnet above shows the generative element of this at work, while 'pre-trained' indicates that it is provided in a condition to work immediately. 'Transformer' refers to the deep learning architecture behind the programme (Smith, 2025). As complex as this sounds, transformers are quite limited, for all that they can produce remarkable content almost instantly. Being built on 'attention modules' they can only reference present contexts (Behrouz et al., 2024). They have no ability to remember over a long period of time. Whenever a transformer carries out a task, it highlights the short string of words or phrases with which it is currently dealing; it is not set up to remember information from lengthy texts and will falter after a few thousand words. In human terms, an equivalent would be trying to write an essay based on ideas held in the head with no recourse to notes, plans or even memory.

The previous section underlined that this is not how human intelligence operates. Rather, the human mind prioritises information that is important, forgets that which is not needed and tends to give prominence to things discovered unexpectedly (Swayne, 2025). The human memory is short term (it can hold information for current use), long term (it can access older information and updates as it encounters new information) and persistent (it retains important information as a background to other learning) (Golabek, 2025). It can retrieve information with particular skill; in a quiz, a person may, without preparation, recall information about a subject that they have not thought about for years.

A new Google-pioneered architecture for LLMs that goes under the name of 'Titan' (Behrouz et al., 2024), promises to bring AI more into line with human modes of thinking (as a side note, it could be mentioned that the subtitle for Shelley's *Frankenstein* is 'The Modern Prometheus', Prometheus being one of the ancient Demi-gods, or Titans, from Greek myth). Titans introduce three innovations that will extend the memory capacity and, hence, processing power, of AI. The first is a long-term neural memory module: Titans will still work, as transformers do, by picking on small pieces of information held in short-term memory, but that information will be given a context of other information stored over a long period. The second is a surprise-based method of learning. Just as humans tend to remember events that they do not expect (such as the plot twist or big reveal in a story), so Titans will be programmed to particularly notice breaks and errors in patterns. The third feature is a loss function. Titans will not be universal memory dumps but masters of a system of knowledge organised for goal-accomplishment and purpose. Data that are not useful will be de-prioritised or deleted (Robison, 2025).

Three memory modes for Titan are envisaged, Memory as Context (MAC), Memory as Gate (MAG) and Memory as Layer (MAL) (Noguer I Alonso, 2025). MAC takes information being read in the present and synthesises it with relevant stored memories. For tasks that demand prior knowledge to effect understanding of current information, this approach will be appropriate. MAG is more editorially astute, making decisions about which stored data, if any, are useful for understanding any given piece of information. This is an efficient way to process data in that it only accesses older material when it needs to do so. MAL veers closer to the way an expert person's mind might work, processing information in the light the totality of what is already known. As should be clear, these Titan variants will each be applicable to different types of tasks, while complementing each other as part of an overall AI application (Lee, 2025).

Such a development would improve AI performance in several important fields. It would be more skilled than transformers at understanding the language that it processed, producing more coherent text. Chatbots, content creation and document analysis would all benefit. A Titan application could also enhance decision-making and forecasting across a range of sectors (such as finance) by analysing time sequences more accurately. Finally, it would have the computational power to sequence genomes flawlessly (Goyal, 2025). It would be a major advance towards the emergence of a fully agentic AI, that is, AI that can make autonomous decisions in the moment with no reference back to any prior command or request (Hughes et al., 2025).

It would also be a solid foundation for 'hybrid' or 'human in the loop' intelligence (Jarvela et al., 2025). Hybrid intelligence, as its name implies, is a putative fusion of human intelligence and AI that would combine the strengths of both. AI outperforms human beings as far as information processing is concerned but is notably poorer in other cognitive and affective modes.

When questions are raised about what AI can do for organisations and society, the answers usually revolve around activities that require reason, rationality and the adherence to set schemas. Beyond the party tricks that amaze users of ChatGPT, AI has the capacity to manage systems, give real world direction, perform complex searches and synthesise not just human words but also human music, human art, even human voices. Lili Ziren is an evocative example of these activities.

What AI cannot do, however, is intuit or play a significant role in scenarios which demand an emotional response (Braga & Logan, 2017). AI has no emotional intelligence (Goleman, 2020). Furthermore, AI has often (although not always) taken a somewhat biased or amoral line (Hanna et al., 2025) when tasked with solving non-binary dilemmas. Since AI is only as good as the data sets from which it has learned – however huge they may have been – there is no guarantee that it will behave ethically. These areas are ones to which human beings are uniquely suited.

Consider, as an example, a fighter pilot flying over enemy territory. AI could control the plane, scan for dangers and initiate counter-measures in the event of the plane being attacked. It would have faster reaction times than any human being. It would not, though, be the best authority as far as judging whether to carry out or abort the mission. It would make its decision based on purely rational factors; only the pilot would have the insight and vision needed to perceive, evaluate and, perhaps, imagine any broader moral implications. Pilot and AI system is a potent combination when they are collaborating; either working alone would be less effective.

2.4 Case Study: A Proto-Hybrid Organisation

Company A is based in the UK and manufactures cooling fans for industrial machinery. It has no standard products, instead designing everything to order. It has customers all around the world. As a business, it is relatively young but growing at a rapid pace. Given the nature of its offer and customer profile, it already makes extensive use of AI and plans to go further.

Much of the AI at present is geared towards the customer experience. When fans need maintenance in different time zones, AI allows for the conveying of detailed guidance whatever the hour in the home country. Since each product is unique, such advice must be specifically tailored. To meet this challenge, the company is building its own AI system on the back of commercially available LLMs, information about its products and their manufacture being used as the raw material for machine learning. This is a process that, at the time of writing, is not over – or close to being over.

As far as making the fans is concerned, AI allows for speedy and super-accurate quality control. Hitherto, stress-testing fans' impellers has been a time-consuming operation that has required huge amounts of data-processing memory and concomitant energy usage. AI cuts the needed time down from hours to minutes. Similarly, fully briefing, training and enculturating product designers has always taken upwards of six months. AI can achieve the same results without the acclimatisation period. Other roles, too, will alter as they become subject to more input from AI.

None of this means that Company A is making people obsolete. The business's leaders envisage AI and people working together. People will still oversee what AI is doing, as well as set the parameters for its activities. People are also the desired main contact for customers. The company has not yet reached the point at which the integration of humans and AI is happening consistently, so as much as it resembles a human-AI hybrid organisation, it would be truer to call it a 'proto-hybrid organisation': its leaders foresee a future in which the human and artificial elements work together but, for now, AI is still a tool, albeit an increasingly useful one.

The company does, though, illustrate the potential for a dynamic interplay of humans and AI. AI is fulfilling its main function of expanding human intelligence. By completing tasks quickly and with a high degree of accuracy, AI is removing 'human error' from the mix while hugely improving productivity. However, it is only helping people perform better; it has not taken over any functions entirely and, for the moment, there is no reason to assume that it will.

The example of Company A brings the argument to a place in which leadership and AI begin to converge. Hybrid intelligence, powered by architectures such as AI Titans, could well become the dominant driver of many, if not most, organisations, all of which will need some form of leadership. That said, having some grasp of the nature of AI is not the same as fully appreciating the impact that it could have: not to be dismissed are the threats as well as the opportunities that it offers to society, organisations and, at the base of both, individuals.

References

Bailey, R. P., Samusuddin, N., Ali, A., Ibrahim, K. F. K., Chan, N. N., Jenatabadi, H. S. & Xu, Y. (2025). Cognitive prosthesis: A post-Cartesian model of technological extension. In press.

Behrouz, A., Zhong, P. & Mirrokni, V. (2024). *Titans: Learning to Memorise at Test Time*. Google Research.

Blank, I. A. (2023). What are large language models supposed to model? *Trends in Cognitive Sciences*, 27(11), 987–989.

Bojic, L., Stojkovic, I. & Marjanovic, Z. J. (2024). Signs of consciousness in AI: Can ChatGPT-3 tell how smart it really is? *Humanities & Social Science Communications*, 11, 1631.

Borg, E. (2025). LLMs, Turing tests and Chinese rooms: The prospects for meaning in league language models. *Inquiry*, 1–31.

Braga, A. & Logan, R. K. (2017). The emperor of strong AI has no clothes: Limits of artificial intelligence. *Information*, 8(4).

Carlson, M. A. (2006). A brief history of the 1987 stock market crash with a discussion of the Federal Reserve response. *Finance and Economics Discussion Series*, 13, 1–24.

Clarke, A. C. (1968). *2001: A Space Odyssey*. Hutchinson.

Giacaglia, G. P. (2021). *Making Things Think*. Holloway.

Golabek, P. (2025). AI that thinks like a human: Titans & transformers2 and the future of adaptive intelligence. *Kubert*, January 30, https://mykubert.com/blog/ai-that-thinks-like-a-human-titans-transformer-squared-and-the-future-of-adaptive-intelligence/ [accessed May 8th 2025].

Goleman, D. (2020). *Emotional Intelligence: Why It Can Matter More Than IQ*. 25th Anniversary Edition. Bloomsbury Publishing.

Goncalves, B. (2023). The Turing Test is a thought experiment. *Minds and Machines*, 33(4), 1–31.

Goyal, M. (2025). Titans: A deep dive into next-generation AI memory architecture. *DEV*, February 4, https://dev.to/mohitgoyal09/titans-a-deep-dive-into-next-generation-ai-memory-architecture-1e7h [accessed May 8th 2025].

Gruetzemacher, R. (2022). The power of natural language processing. *Harvard Business Review*, April 19th 2022, https://hbr.org/2022/04/the-power-of-natural-language-processing [accessed Sunday 21st September 2025].

Ha, T. & Kim, S. (2024). Improving trust in AI with mitigating confirmation bias: Effects of explanation type and debiasing strategy for decision-making with explainable AI. *International Journal of Human-Computer Interaction*, 40(24), 8562–8573.

Haddy, E., Burden, F., Raw, Z., Rodrigues, J. B., Zappi Bello, J. H., Brown, J., Kaminski, J. & Proops, L. (2023). Belief in animal sentience and affective owner attitudes are linked to positive working equip welfare across six countries. *Journal of Applied Animal Welfare*, 28(1), 116–134.

Hanna, M. G., Pantanowitz, L., Jackson, B., Palmer, O., Visweswaran, S., Pantanowitz, J., Deebajah, M. & Rashidi, H. H. (2025). Ethical and bias considerations in artificial intelligence/machine learning. *Modern Pathology*, 38(3), 1–13.

Hughes, L., Dwivedi, Y. K., Malik, T., Shawosh, M., Albashwari, M. A., Dutot, I. J. V., Appanderanda, M., Crick, T., De', R., Fenwick, M., Gunaratnege, S. M., Jurcys, P., Kar, A. K., Kshetri, N., Li, K., Mutasa, S., Samthrakis, S., Wade, M. & Walton, P. (2025). AI and agentic systems: A multi-expert analysis. *Journal of Computer Information Systems*, 1–29.

Iqbal, S. (2024). The intelligence spectrum: Unravelling the path from ANI to ASI. *Journal of Computing & Biomedical Informatics*, 7(2), 1–28.

Jarrahi, M. H., Lutz, C. & Newlands, G. (2022). Artificial intelligence, human intelligence and hybrid intelligence based on mutual augmentation. *Big Data & Society*, 9(2).

Jarvela, S., Zhao, G., Nguyen, A. & Chen, H. (2025). *British Journal of Educational Technology*, 56(2), 455–468.

Korteling, J. E. H., van de Boer-Visschedijk, G. C., Blankendaal, R. A. M., Boonekamp, R. C. & Eikelboom, A. R. (2021). Human- versus artificial intelligence. *Frontiers in Artificial Intelligence*, 4, 622364, doi:10.3389/frai.2021.622364.

Lee, R. (2025). *Natural Language Processing*. Springer.

Legg, S. & Hutter, M. (2007). Universal intelligence: A definition of machine intelligence. *Minds & Machines*, 17, 391–444.

Lerner, J. S., Li, Y., Valdesolo, P. & Kassam, K. S. (2015). Emotion and decision making. *The Annual Review of Psychology*, 66, 799–823.

Losey, R. (2024). Artificial general intelligence, if attained, will be the greatest invention of all time. *EDRM Blog*, https://edrm.net/2024/08/artificial-general-intelligence-if-attained-will-be-the-greatest-invention-of-all-time/ [accessed May 5th 2025].

Mitchell, M. (2024). The Turing Test and our shifting conceptions of intelligence. *Science*, 385(6710).

Mugaanyi, J., Cai, L., Cheng, S., Lu, C. & Huang, J. (2024). Evaluation of large language model performance and reliability for citations and references in scholarly writing: Cross-disciplinary study. *Journal of Medical Internet Research*, 26.

Murgia, M. (2024). *Code Dependent: How AI Is Changing Our Lives*. Picador.

Noguer I Alonso, M. (2025). *Transformer Squared and Titans: The Mathematics*. SSRN, https://papers.ssrn.com/sol3/papers.cfm?abstract_id=5100305 [accessed September 21st 2025].

Pinker, S. (2010). The cognitive niche: Coevolution of intelligence, sociality and language. In J. C. Avis & F. J. Ayala (Eds.), *In the Light of Evolution: Volume IV: The Human Condition*. National Academies Press.

Poole, J. (2025). AGI in 2025: Are we already past Kurzweil's singularity? Medium, April 3rd 2025, https://medium.com/@jp180j/agi-in-2025-are-we-already-past-kurzweils-singularity-befe93636e3c [accessed Sunday September 21st 2025].

Raiaan, A. K. R., Mukta, M. S. H., Fatema, K., Fahd, N. M., Sakib, S. & Mim, M. M. J. (2024). A review on Large Language Models: Architectures, applications, taxonomies, open issues and challenges. *IEEE Access*, 12, 26839–26874.

Robison, G. (2025). DeepMind's Titans: Teaching AI to remember like humans. Medium, January 16th 2025, https://gregrobison.medium.com/deepminds-titans-teaching-ai-to-remember-like-humans-6ba606094668 [accessed September 21st 2025]

Salovey, P. & Mayer, J. D. (1990). Emotional intelligence. *Imagination, Cognition and Personality*, 9(3), 185–211.

Saranya, A. & Subhashini, R. (2023). A systematic review of Explainable Artificial Intelligence models and applications: Recent developments and future trends. *Decision Analytics Journal*, 7(5), 100230.

Searle, J. (1999). The Chinese room. In R. A. Wilson & F. Keil (Eds.), *The MIT Encyclopedia of the Cognitive Sciences*. MIT Press.

Smith, C. S. (2025). Google's Titans give AI human-like memory. Forbes, January 21st 2025, https://www.forbes.com/sites/craigsmith/2025/01/19/googles-titans-give-ai-human-like-memory/ [accessed September 21st 2025]

Swayne, M. (2025). Google's 'Titans' models offer a scalable memory system for AI. *AI Insider*, https://theaiinsider.tech/2025/01/16/googles-titans-models-offer-a-scalable-memory-system-for-ai/ [accessed May 5th 2025].

Toon, N. (2024). *How AI Thinks*. Random House.

Turing, A. M. (1950). Computing machinery and intelligence. *Mind*, LIX, 433–460.

Van Kleef, G. A. & Cote, S. (2022). The social effects of emotions. *Annual Review of Psychology*, 73, 629–658.

Van Vugt, M. (2006). Evolutionary origins of leadership and followership. *Personality and Social Psychology Review*, 10(4), 354–371.

Walsh, C. (2020). What the nose knows. The Harvard Gazette, February 27th 2020, https://news.harvard.edu/gazette/story/2020/02/how-scent-emotion-and-memory-are-intertwined-and-exploited/ [accessed September 21st 2025].

Youssef, A., Stein, S., Clapp, J. & Magnus, D. (2023). The importance of understanding language in large language models. *The American Journal of Bioethics*, 23(10), 6–7.

3 AI Opportunities and Threats

3.1 Introduction

Artificial Intelligence (AI) may or may not be conscious but it is becoming more and more autonomous (Bernath, 2021). Irrespective of whether it meets the Chinese Room or Imitation Game standard for intelligence, tools are being developed that will give it greater decision-making power such that it could ultimately require little or no human supervision (Hughes et al., 2025). This raises ethical concerns about control and accountability, as well as having practical implications for how organisations delegate authority, manage risk and design decision-making structures.

Before going further, it is important to distinguish between ‘agentic AI’ and ‘AI agents’. AI agents are already becoming a part of the business ecosystem. They have been developed to perform specific tasks and despite being capable of executing decisions, they still need human input and oversight. Examples would include customer service chatbots and interfaces such as Apple’s Siri or Amazon’s Alexa. Agentic AI refers to a more systemic programme that is capable of running entire functions with no human involvement. The technology is still in its early stages of development but is already to be found in areas such as supply chain management and healthcare.

AI with agentic qualities is not new. In one sense, so-called multi-agency systems (MAS) have demonstrated a form of agency for a long time (Coulter, 2022). An MAS consists of many actors – which could be computer programmes or just lines of computer code – all with different agendas that bond together to attain common goals or carry out some other activity of shared significance. AI agency is merely this process taken further and given an architecture – which could be transformers or Titans. With AI, the improvements in autonomy are startling, LLMs having shown signs of emergent behaviours ahead of what would be expected from their programming. How far this is a sign of intelligence or sentience is another discussion (Floridi, 2024).

Again, there is a spectrum to the probable applications of AI agency. At one end, it may make decisions constantly in the background unnoticed by, and with no interference from, human beings. At the other end, humans will

DOI: 10.4324/9781003665533-3

be empowered to act should AI be inclined to behave in a way that is deemed detrimental or immoral. In the longer term, the risk that an AGI could break free of human control altogether and become entirely self-determining is viewed by some as so serious that 'scalable oversight' – whereby a weak AI monitors and, if necessary, blocks, a strong AI – is in active development (Engels et al., 2025).

Whether or not the fear is realistic, agentic AI is predicted to become a significant element in the organisations of the future (Bucaile et al., 2024). There is still a considerable distance between LLMs and their architectures – even Titans – and fully agentic AGI, meaning that activities which are clearly delineated in terms of process and outcome are those that will likely be affected first (Coshow et al., 2024). For all the opportunity, though, there is jeopardy on macro- as well as micro-levels (Ajami & Karimi, 2023). As alluded to at the start of this chapter, ethics, trust and even identity will be tested as agentic AI becomes ever more prevalent, presenting considerable challenges to leaders at all levels of organisations and society.

3.2 Society

AI offers society as a whole the chance to address, if not solve, some of its most pressing and complex problems (OECD, 2019). AI is capable of producing powerful predictive models, albeit that results have, to date, been mixed. Climate change, for example, is an area in which scientists have tested 'emulator' AIs and 'foundational models' that eschew overly mathematical approaches in favour of naturalistic designs (Wong, 2024). Not all findings have been convincing, but the direction of travel is undeniable: AI models will continue to grow in accuracy, influencing policymaking and research. In a similar vein, food security can be enhanced by AI that monitors crops, identifies pests and controls for erratic weather conditions (Sharma, 2024). Healthcare stands to be improved; studies have shown that AI improves, *inter alia*, cancer detection, diabetes management, heart disease detection and the treatment of neurological disorders. It also has high potential in healthcare administration and management (Varnosfaderani & Farouzanfar, 2024). It need hardly be said that AI's effect on wealth, as well as health, is predicted to be substantial and positive, with some USD 15.7 trillion to be added to the global economy by 2030. This sounds like a huge gain but not all sectors or geographies will benefit to the same extent (Gonzales, 2023).

None of this is to suggest that AI will be purely a public good. A major challenge that it poses is for inclusion and equity (Qian et al., 2024). As has already been mentioned, machine and deep learning are far from neutral processes. LLMs have been shown to be prone to class, race and gender biases. Not only have they reproduced – and sometimes amplified – representational harms, such as derogatory language, exclusionary norms and stereo-typing, but they have been found to discriminate in practical situations, as when they have been used in application screening for jobs and shown clear partiality for members of certain groups (Gallegos et al., 2024). A study by Ayoub et al (2024) charged a Chatbot with imagining itself as a physician with specific demographic characteristics before setting it a series of questions around the allocation of scarce medical resources. The findings identified a marked tendency for the algorithms to favour 'their' people. Although the research dealt with hypothetical situations, the implication is that decisions made by AI agents could have severe real-world consequences.

On the one hand, this is to debunk the claim that AI is close to any kind of general intelligence: in these instances, AI has simply been a filter for the material used in its training. On the other, it invites a discussion around the ethical and moral position of AI as an autonomous entity. In legal terms, this is to pose the problem of agentic AI 'personhood' (Forrest, 2024).

If, as an example, a car driven by an agentic AI system knocks down and kills a pedestrian, who is to blame for that person's death? It could be put down to an 'act of God' but that is to create the kind of vacuum that the law abhors. The AI may have acted *ultra vires*, giving the owner reasonable deniability. The same would be true for the manufacturer. Unless the car's code has been in some way tampered with, the manufacturer could abjure all responsibility. The insurer Hiscox UK has already taken into account the possibility of legal action arising from such a case by creating products that indemnify companies against possible AI-related claims (Scott, 2025).

Perhaps, in the example, blame should be ascribed to the AI that was driving the car. Saying this is to beg the type of question that fuels the academic article industry, but it is pertinent to do so, especially as AI has been found, in some circumstances, to be more adept at moral judgements than has hitherto been believed. As Dillion et al (2025) demonstrate, when presented with complex dilemmas, or multiple moral choices of equal merit, AI has outperformed renowned ethicists by reaching conclusions preferred by research participants. If AI is morally aware, there is a strong case for its being morally – and legally – culpable.

Forcing AI to face its responsibilities – in effect, acknowledging its personhood – means that it should also be granted its due rights (Rao, 2024). This may seem absurd, but animal rights are a reality and the difference between animals and AI is not as great as may be thought. Despite being conscious, most animals display no signs of human-like intelligence, whereas AI, despite not being conscious, does. If animals have rights, why should AI not? Why should a person in a persistent vegetative state have rights and AI not? When machines are nothing more than a technical means to accomplish a given task, the question is not worth answering, but something that is agentic and autonomous may be owed a duty of care. How that duty would be enforced is currently indeterminate: could an AI ever be a plaintiff in a civil case? Some argue that to even ask is to devalue humanity by assigning it to a technology that is not provably sentient (Rao, 2024). Either way, such issues will, sooner or later, need to be confronted by society. They will also need to be uppermost in the minds of organisational leaders since they will have a bearing on what is meant by 'organisational members'. Should the personhood of AI ever be established, the natural corollary will be to grant it employment rights – with concomitant responsibilities for organisations and their leaders (McKinsey & Company, 2025).

3.3 Organisations

The world is in the midst of 4IR – the Fourth Industrial Revolution – and heading towards 5IR – the Fifth iteration of the same (Adel, 2022). The terminology implies continuity, but it disguises the need for radical shifts in mindset. Whereas previous 'industrial revolutions' have prioritised efficiency and the effective exploitation of resources, the fifth will place a higher value on wellbeing and sustainability (Ali et al., 2022). At its heart will be technology, especially AI, and its relationship with human beings (Noble et al., 2022); human–AI hybrid organisations will be a central feature. This means that the opportunities and threats around AI for organisations – in both public and private sectors – are of paramount importance.

The IT-based management consultancy Gartner prepared a report on AI in 2024 that made several bold predictions about the potential of agentic AI to revolutionalise business in coming years (Coshow et al., 2024). By the close of the 2020s, it stated, 33% of business software applications would include agentic AI, agentic AI would account for 20% of interactions that customers would have with digital shopfronts and, most surprisingly, agentic AI would make 15% of the average business's day-to-day decisions. Since AI can analyse datasets and proceed to action at speed, the effort currently spent on making decisions can be considerably reduced. Performance gains across functions should result (Coshow et al., 2024).

Decision-making will no longer occur only during a 'working day'. Security concerns that arise overnight, movements in markets in different time zones and news that an advertising campaign needs to be tweaked can all be responded to in real time at any moment in the 24-hour cycle. Machine learning algorithms enable nuanced forecasting of demand by analysing current and historic market data: inventories can thus be adjusted in real time to their optimal levels for particular trading conditions (Taylor, 2025). Prices can be set realistically in the light of such information.

In that many of the decisions made by AI will be around structured activities rather than strategies, firms will have the chance to adopt flatter organisational designs by removing middle leadership and management roles (Hughes et al., 2025). Whether they should and what it might mean for the people who lose their jobs will be explored later. For the moment, a caution should be noted to the effect that predictions about what AI can achieve are often speculative and assume advances in technology that are embryonic, or at the conceptual stage. Supply chain risk management, for example, is ripe for the application of AI, but until recently older mathematical models were still being used by most companies (Baryannis et al., 2019).

The customer experience is already being enhanced by AI and it will continue to be so. Conversations with customer service chatbots are now an everyday event for consumers, but soon those conversations will include not only standard replies lifted from a set menu but entirely new sentences generated for the occasion – natural language, in other words. Such conversations will be informed by the vastly more detailed market information recoverable by AI. Purchase decisions having been made, shipping and delivery to customers will be more reliable. Alibaba and Amazon are two companies that manage the millions of parcels that they send every week using AI software and robotics (Zhang et al., 2021). With AI-powered drones as the method of delivery, humans are increasingly being left out of the loop.

Outlining what AI can do for organisations is inadvertently to hint at the negatives. Perhaps the biggest is that it may all be nonsense. History is littered with moments when a new disruptive technology has been touted as a game changer for work, production processes and the amount of time that could be devoted to leisurely pursuits (Spencer, 2023) only for it to disappoint in practice. The number of hours that people work has fallen substantially over the last century, but the trend has been the same in all countries, irrespective of their technological level (Rasmussen, 2024). Restrictive policies have had as much to do with the changes as technological progress. Despite this, surveys confirm that workers often feel that they are busier and more pressured than ever – even when, from an objective perspective, they are not (O'Connor, 2022). Technology has done nothing to make them feel that their lives are any easier.

This is only one example. More generally, technology has alleviated but not eliminated the problems of the past and there is no guarantee that AI will fare any better. It is possible, then, that AI may be incorporated into current routines, its capacities either underutilised, or used in ways that fail to make much difference to occupational environments. Research has found that the same AI placed into different organisations has produced radically divergent outcomes (Bankins et al., 2023); this would not be expected were AI making genuinely impactful decisions. Instead, it implies that AI is being used as a tool in the same manner as previous generations of ICT, its full scope remaining unexplored. Research by the consultancy firm Accenture (Narain et al., 2024) found that only 13% of executives are 'extremely confident' in their ability to make the most of AI.

Other dangers around AI for organisations are more immediate. Inadequate AI equipment could be harmful to businesses, but so could poor quality data. If AI's inputs are insufficient, it will not make an optimum contribution to productivity. At present, customer service bots are among the most noticeable commercial AIs. Should they provide bad service or be viewed as too impersonal, they may be rejected by customers, leading to demands for human-only customer interactions (Coshow et al., 2024). Such a desire for older technologies with which people can connect emotionally and culturally might be called 'the vinyl effect': vinyl records are more primitive in every respect than other music platforms, but their popularity has increased in recent years as they have been re-embraced by customers who value their more tactile and analogue qualities.

It is not, though, only companies' communications with their customers that could be adversely affected. B2B (business-to-business) interactions carry the risk of misunderstandings arising as companies' AI makes use of information about collaborators not curated from business relationships – which could consequently turn sour (Papagiannidis et al., 2023). Ultimately, the dilemma facing organisations is that allowing AI to make their decisions – or some of their decisions – is only desirable if those decisions are deemed to be the correct ones: what happens when people in organisations do not agree with them?

3.3.1 Case Study: AI for Decision-Making

A good exemplar of the opportunities and threats discussed above would be a business organisation that can be called Company B. Headquartered in the UK, but with remote offices in various countries, including Canada and the USA, it describes itself as being in the business of decision intelligence. This means that it helps managers from its client firms make better decisions and, thus, achieve improved performance from their human employees. The clients are mostly banks and health insurance companies. A typical decision of the type handled by Company B would be about the planning of capacity to optimise workflows and give a boost to productivity. This would come from a perception that time is being wasted because of mismatches between resourcing capacity and improved service. Other decisions might be around objectives or targets being set for the company or individuals within it, or the need to build skills in specific areas and so on. On a more granular level, managers might even be briefed on what to say in specific situations, including one-to-one meetings. Although the client list includes financial firms, the advice given is not generally numerical and statistical in nature; instead, it is a mixture of the strategic and the tactical.

Company B's role is to collect relevant data, process it and then generate an appropriate decision, often with ideas around how to communicate it. Originally, this was done by the company's human employees, then simple IT packages took over and now the main vehicle is AI. The company is clear that they are not providing training or consultancy but embedding a way of working focused on augmenting the human decision-making process. The most common request from clients unable to cope with a large amount of data is simply: tell us what to do! Company B is actually very careful about how it reacts in such instances. For low-grade operations that could be fully automated, it makes a single decision that is then effectively imposed on its clients. For bigger decisions that may affect lives or livelihoods, a range of options is presented to senior managers who then have to choose which best fits their priorities.

This *modus operandi* has a number of implications. Firstly, it acknowledges moral fuzziness. Senior leader decisions are not consequence-free and are not to be taken lightly. A healthcare company could be asked to make a decision that leads to someone's death. AI should not be entrusted with it in the absence of checks and balances (this is a topic which will be returned to in the next chapter). Secondly, projecting into the future, Company B's interventions give further confirmation of the threatened demise of middle management. The uncomplicated decisions are those that would normally be made by middle managers. The work of Company B would seem to be engendering a future in which organisations will consist of senior leaders making strategic calls picked from AI-generated options and people at the lowest levels interacting with customers and performing mechanical tasks – with everything in the middle done by AI alone. However, that the situation is more complex will be discussed in a later chapter.

3.4 Individuals

The increasing penetration of AI into all areas of modern life heralds the onset of an age of 'hyper-personalisation' (Ziesche & Yampolskiy, 2025). Content is increasingly susceptible of being tailored precisely to individual consumers' needs, using demographic data and analyses of expressed preferences. Even today, visitors to social networks and similar are familiar with content that reflects browsing histories – and attendant concerns around privacy (Karami et al., 2024). Hyper-personalisation also applies to hitherto human-only interactions, such as those with health care workers, teachers and so on; in the future, illnesses will be diagnosed in seconds and student performance will be assessable in real time using AI marking tools (Ziesche & Yampolskiy, 2025). Hyper-personalisation will be a key element of the Fifth Industrial Revolution (Ziatdinov et al., 2024).

In occupational terms, a major benefit of AI is the extent to which workers lives are improved by natural language's ability to simplify the management of complex processes and projects (Coshow et al., 2024). From accounting to design to record-keeping, tasks that have traditionally been time-consuming and difficult are made easier by the addition of AI. In education, to take one area, this is bringing benefits in terms of planning and research, but at the cost of much angst around learning and assessment. Throughout the stages of schooling, but particularly in higher education, controversies are raging over what rules and boundaries need to be set for the use of AI by students. Since ChatGPT can produce a piece of argumentative and analytical writing in moments, the implications for genuine scholarship are grave. Academics are divided on how to respond: some advocate for a return to set-piece examinations, or, at least, an insistence on work being hand-written; others accept AI for what it is and look for ways in which it can help students produce better pieces of work (Wise et al., 2024).

Not all AI is the same in this regard. Students who study in a second language often use packages such as Grammarly to add elegance to their writing: they can hardly be accused of 'cheating'. Even those who use ChatGPT and its like to write their work in its entirety need to provide the programme with parameters (Marzuki et al., 2023). This is intellectual work. Indeed, it could validly be claimed that it is where learning really occurs. AI might be applying literary gloss, but it is not doing the hard graft of gaining knowledge.

The point is that, in this case, AI is not replacing human input but simply augmenting and improving it. That is not to say that concerns around deskilling can be blithely dismissed. As AI develops its capabilities, certain occupations will lose much of their status and purpose (Dahlin, 2024). Up to 60% of jobs will fundamentally change due to AI by 2030 (Kelly, 2025). AI can already process financial data more quickly, more efficiently and more accurately than any human bookkeeper. Continuous auditing allows for the production of 'evergreen reports' that show a snapshot of a business on demand with no need for occasional stock takes (Hasan, 2022). Management and chartered accountants could thus find themselves becoming little more than spectators in their own professions. Much the same is true of administrators and copywriters – to give just two other examples.

Such situations have psychological as well as professional ramifications. Professional identities are at hazard of being eroded. Insofar as professional identity is a key part of peoples' – for want of a better word – personhood, the effects on wellbeing could be severe (Selenko et al., 2022). Previous cycles of technological advancement have tended to hit practical and lower skilled workers. Factory machinery affected those in traditional trades. Modern modes of transport and containerisation were devastating for drivers and dockworkers. AI, by contrast, is a disruptor to professions that have largely been insulated from the effects of new ways of doing things (Sharps et al, 2024). It is true that an accountant uses a laptop where their predecessors would have consulted ledgers, but the knowledge involved is the same: no one has suggested that professional qualifications are less rigorous than they have ever been. AI is changing this. Commentators are predicting the rise of a 'useless class' of people with training and skills that AI has rendered to all intents and purposes obsolete; the World Economic Forum has predicted the loss of 85 million jobs to AI worldwide by the end of 2025 (Russo, 2020), although there would be new jobs in occupations connected to AI, or in areas that would exploit its potential.

Only so much comfort should be taken from this: the 'great deleveraging', as it has been called, is actually the tipping point at which increases in productivity due to AI will destroy jobs more quickly than new jobs can be created (Kelly, 2025). For those suddenly made unemployed, there is a tendency to develop 'learned helplessness', which is a condition of lethargy and apathy arising from repeated failure and rejection (Morrison, 2025). Notwithstanding the fact that AI-driven unemployment has not, so far, been noted on a significant scale, forecasts suggest that the long-term trend is upwards. This presents a challenge for leaders of both organisations and society: what is to be done about the possibly huge numbers of economically inactive, burned out, people who will make up a sizeable proportion of the working-age population of tomorrow?

In plain terms, AI is a great leveler. Where intelligence has always been seen as a differentiator of people – as well as the passkey to certain professions – it will no longer enjoy such high status. As has been seen, much that has previously been unique to human intelligence – memory, analytical skills, creativity – can now be outsourced to an infinitely faster and more efficient AI agent. This will provoke a major shift in social attitudes. The human qualities that will be most highly valued will be those that cannot easily be handed over to AI, such as empathy, an arm around the shoulder, a few words of comfort, and so on. The people who are masters of these will be the winners in the age of AI; it need hardly be reiterated that this will cause changes to styles of leadership.

3.5 Conclusion

The central theme of this discussion is that AI agents and agentic AI, when used as tools, present major opportunities, but bringing them into a relationship with people is to invite problems. Much of this springs from society, organisations and individuals lacking the moral and intellectual maturity to integrate new forms of intelligence smoothly. This is not a criticism. A technology as novel and – at least potentially – as powerful as AI cannot but be a challenge to established thought patterns and modes of behaviour. It will take some adjusting to. Segregation of people and AI would neither be practical nor desirable – the whole point of technology is to make human life better. The precise proportions of human intelligence and AI in a human–AI hybrid organisation, therefore, will need careful consideration. There will, no doubt, be 'teething troubles' and 'false starts' on the road to an optimal balance being struck.

These issues have implications for all people, but they are particularly relevant to leaders. How leaders handle them will largely determine the extent to which the opportunities are taken advantage of and the threats avoided. It should be clear that, whatever happens, leadership cannot remain unaffected: it will need to adapt to a world that is itself in constant flux. As the case study in this chapter indicates, fully agentic AI is still to have noticeable influence on the ways in which organisations run. Nevertheless, that it will arrive at some point is a near-certainty – and with it will come the fully human–AI hybrid organisation. Agentic AI is, of course, only one half of the equation and how comfortably the human element can accept and assimilate it will be crucial to the success or otherwise of such human–AI hybrid organisations.

References

Adel, A. (2022). Future of Industry 5.0 in society: Human-centric solutions, challenges and prospective research areas. *Journal of Cloud Computing*, 11(40).

Ajami, R. A. & Karimi, H. A. (2023). Artificial intelligence: Opportunities and challenges. *Journal of Asia-Pacific Business*, 24(2), 73–75.

Ali, S. H., Al-Sultan, H. A. & Al Rubaie, M. T. (2022). Fifth industrial revolution: (New perspectives). *International Journal of Business, Management and Economics*, 3(3), 196–212.

Ayoub, N. F., Balakrishnan, K., Ayoub, M. S., Barrett, T. F., David, A. P. & Gray, S. T. (2024). Inherent bias in learners language models: A random sampling analysis. *Mayo Clinical Proceedings: Digital Health*, 2(2), 186–191.

Bankins, S., Ocampo, A. C., Marrone, M., Restubog, S. L. D. & Woo, S. E. (2023). A multilevel review of artificial intelligence in organisatinos: Implications for organisational behaviour research and practice. *Journal of Organisational Behavior*, 45(7), 159–182.

Baryannis, G., Validi, S., Dani, S. & Antoniou, G. (2019). Supply chain risk management and artificial intelligence: State of the art and future research directions. *International Journal of Production Research*, 57(7), 2179–2202.

Bernath, L. (2021). Can autonomous agents without phenomenal consciousness be morally responsible? *Philosophy & Technology*, 34, 1363–1382.

Bucaille, A., Westcott, K., Crossan, G. & Abrash, L. (2024). TMT predictions 2025: Bridging the gaps. *Deloitte*, https://www2.deloitte.com/us/en/insights/industry/technology/technology-media-and-telecom-predictions.html [accessed Thursday May 8th 2025].

Coshow, T., Gao, A., Pingree, L., Verma, A., Shcheibenreif, D., Khandabattu, H. & Olliffe, G. (2024). Top strategic technology trends for 2025: Agentic AI. *Gartner*, https://www.gartner.com/doc/reprints?id=1-2K8Y7LEY&ct=250212&st=sb

Coulter, D. A. (2022). The convergence of computational thinking, computational intelligence and multi-agency. *Journal of Integrated Design and Process Science*, 26(3-4), 369–391.

Dahlin, E. (2024). Who says artificial intelligence is stealing our jobs? *Socius: Sociological Research for a Dynamic World*, 10.

Dillion, D., Mondal, D., Tandon, N. & Gray, K. (2025). AI language model rivals expert ethicist in perceived moral expertise. *Scientific Reports*, 15, 4084.

Engels, J., Baek, D. D., Kantamneni, S. & Tegmark, M. (2025). Scaling laws for scalable oversight. *arXiv* preprint arXiv: 2504.18530.

Floridi, L. (2024). AI as agency without intelligence: On artificial intelligence as a new form of artificial agency and the multiple realisability of agency thesis. *Philosophy & Technology*, 38(30).

Forrest, K. B. (2024). The ethics and challenges of legal personhood for AI. *The Yale Law Journal*, 133, 2023–2024.

Gallegos, I. O., Rossi, R. A., Barrow, J., Tanjim, M. M., Kim, S., Dernancourt, F., Yu, T., Zhang, R. & Ahmed, N. K. (2024). Bias and fairness in large language models: A survey. *Computational Linguistics*, 50(3), 1097–1179.

Gonzales, J. T. (2023). Implications of AI innovation on economic growth: A panel data study. *Journal of Economic Structures*, 12(13). doi.org/10.1186/s40008-023-00307-w.

Hasan, A. R. (2022). Artificial intelligence (AI) in accounting & auditing: A literature review. *Open Journal of Business and Management*, 10(1), 440–465.

Hughes, L., Dwivedi, Y. K., Malik, T., Shawosh, M., Albashwari, M. A., Dutot, I. J. V., Appanderanda, M., Crick, T., De', R., Fenwick, M., Gunaratnege, S. M., Jurcys, P., Kar, A. K., Kshetri, N., Li, K., Mutasa, S., Samthrakis, S., Wade, M. & Walton, P. (2025). AI and agentic systems: A multi-expert analysis. *Journal of Computer Information Systems*, 65(4), 489–517.

Karami, A., Shemshaki, M. & Ghazanfar, M. A. (2024). Exploring the ethical Implications of AI-powered personalisation in digital marketing. *Data Intelligence*, September 2024.

Kelly, J. (2025). These jobs will fall first as AI takes over the workplace. *Forbes*, April 25th.

Marzuki, Widiati, U., Rusdin, D., Darwin & Indrawati, I. (2023). The impact of AI writing tools on the content and organisation of students' writing: EFL teachers' perspective. *Cogent Education*, 10(2), doi.org/10.1080/2331186X.2023.2236469.

McKinsey & Company (2025). The future of work is agentic. Podcast, https://www.mckinsey.com/capabilities/people-and-organizational-performance/our-insights/the-future-of-work-is-agentic [accessed 9th July 2025].

Morrison, E. (2025). Surviving within artificial intelligence's useless class. *Psychology Today*, February 11th, https://www.psychologytoday.com/za/blog/word-less/202502/surviving-within-artificial-intelligences-useless-class/amp [accessed September 21st 2025].

Narain, K., Daugherty, P., Schelfaut, K., Wood, D., Shukla, P. P. & Wilson, J. (2024). *Reinventing with a Digital Core*. Accenture.

Noble, S. M., Mende, M., Grewal, D. & Parasuraman, A. (2022). The fifth Industrial revolution: How harmonious human-machine collaboration is triggering a retail and service [r]evolution. *Journal of Retailing*, 98(2), 199–208.

O'Connor, S. (2022). We're all working harder than ever with nothing but exhaustion to show for it. *Financial Times*, June 10th.

OECD (2019). *Artificial Intelligence in Society*. OECD Publishing.

Papagiannidis, E., Mikalef, P., Conboy, K. & Van de Wetering, R. (2023). Uncovering the dark side of AI-based decision-making: A case study in a B2B context. *Industrial Marketing Management*, 115, 253–265.

Qian, Y., Siau, K. L. & Nah, F. F. (2024). Societal impacts of artificial intelligence: Ethical, legal and governmental issues. *Societal Impacts*, 3.

Rao, D. (2024). Should AI have rights? The Week, May 7th, https://theweek.com/tech/ai-rights-technology-artificial-intelligence [accessed September 21st 2025].

Rasmussen, M. B. (2024). The great standardisation: Working hours around the world. *Labor History*, 65(4), 563–591.

Russo, A. (2020). *Recession and Automation Changes Our Future of Work, but There Are Jobs Coming, Report Says*. World Economic Forum.

Scott, H. (2025). Hiscox UK enhances technology insurance with explicit AI claims coverage. Insurance Times, June 6th, https://www.insurancetimes.co.uk/news/hiscox-uk-enhances-technology-insurance-with-explicit-ai-claims-coverage/1455432.article [accessed September 21st 2025].

Selenko, E., Bankins, S., Shoss, M., Warburton, J. & Restubog, S. L. D. (2022). Artificial intelligence and the future of work: A functional-identity perspective. *Current Directions in Psychological Science*, 31(3), 272–279.

Sharma, S. (2024). Benefits or concerns of AI: A multistakeholder responsibility. *Futures*, 157.

Sharps, S., Smith, T., Browne, J., Large, O., Subramanya, R., Tay, P., Ellington, D., Atkinson, I., Lythgow, J. & Muralidharan, R. (2024). *The Impact of AI on the Labour Market*. Tony Blair Institute for Global Change.

Spencer, D. A. (2023). Technology and work: Past lessons and future directions. *Technology in Society*, 74.

Taylor, A. (2025). How Amazon Business and Alibaba are transforming B2B wholesale with AI. Cleverence.com, https://www.cleverence.com/articles/business-blogs/how-amazon-business-and-alibaba-are-transforming-b2b-wholesale-with-ai/ [accessed May 14th 2025].

Varnosfaderani, S. M. & Farouzanfar, M. (2024). The role of AI in hospitals and clinics: Transforming healthcare in the 21st century. *Bioengineering (Basel)*, 11(4), 337.

Wise, B., Emerson, L., Van Luyn, A., Dyson, B., Bjerknes, C. & Thomas, S. E. (2024). A scholarly dialogue: Writing scholarship, authorship, academic integrity and the challenges of AI. *Higher Education Research & Development*, 43(3), 578–590.

Wong, C. (2024). How AI is improving climate forecasts. *Nature*, 628, 710–712.

Zhang, D., Pee, L. G. & Cui, L. (2021). Artificial intelligence in e-commerce fulfilment: A case study of resource orchestration at Alibaba's smart warehouse. *International Journal of Information Management*, 57(4), 102304

Ziatdinov, R., Atteraya, M. S. & Nabiyev, R. (2024). The fifth industrial revolution as a transformative step towards society 5.0. *Societies*, 14(19).

Ziesche, S. & Yampolskiy, R. V. (2025). Mapping the potential AI-driven hyper-personalised ikigai universe. In S. Ziesche & R. V. Yampolskiy (Eds.), *Considerations on the AI Endgame: Ethics, Risks and Computational Frameworks*. CRC Press.

4 AI Resistance

4.1 Defining AI Resistance

Anxiety about, and resistance to, technology has a long history. The Luddites in early nineteenth century England notoriously smashed machinery that they regarded as a threat to their livelihoods (Charitsis et al., 2025), although they were only one manifestation of a wider feeling of unease, of which *Frankenstein* is, on one reading, a reflection. Artificial Intelligence (AI) is a modern equivalent of the innovations that were so triggering to Shelley and the textile workers who took hammers to power looms: its potential to remodel society is as profound as the Industrial Revolution through which they lived (Makridakis, 2017). Acceptance is no more universal now than it was back then, with AI resistance being widespread.

Broadly, AI resistance is of two types: resistance to AI as a technology and resistance to what AI can do. These may sound similar, if not identical, but they are divergent phenomena that demand different responses. They lie behind the three cognitive domains of AI resistance identified by Golgeci et al (2025): fear, inefficacy and antipathy. Fear and inefficacy touch on resistance to what AI can do. Fear is essentially modern Luddism – anxiety about being replaced in one's job by a machine. Inefficacy is a real or perceived ineptitude when interacting with AI. It has its origins in workers lacking adequate skills to operate with AI or possessing skills that are no longer needed in a world of ever-more sophisticated AI. The third domain, antipathy, is directed more towards AI itself. It is located in worries around trust and privacy, as well as more existential concerns around the impact of AI on identity and relationships. It also bears on the problem of inequity (Shams et al., 2025); cultural objections follow from the sense that AI is serving some groups at the expense of others. Advocacy organisations such as PauseAI propound a version of AI resistance. While there is no suggestion that they condone the Luddites' methods, they are in a line of succession from them.

In discussing AI resistance, it is worth remembering that attitudes change. The Luddites' campaign was short-lived and the notion of AI normalisation was mentioned in the previous chapter. Zehnle et al (2025) have likewise

DOI: 10.4324/9781003665533-4

found that AI resistance is alleviated over time. In part, this is indeed because people become accustomed to AI being part of their lives, but the process is promoted when certain conditions are present. In order to describe what these might be, it is worth looking in more detail at some of the areas that lead to AI resistance.

4.2 Explainability and Trust

Much of the AI currently in use is of the 'black box' variety (Raz et al., 2024). This means that while the inputs into it are clear and its outputs usually comprehensible, the means by which the former are turned into the latter are mysterious. This follows from LLMs' deep learning: the levels of comparison and prediction that it involves take it far from the relatively simple 'if, then' approach of expert systems. The upshot is that even its own developers are often unable to explain the processes that AI has gone through in producing a particular output (Hassija et al., 2024). A related problem is interpretability, or the extent to which people can understand the outputs themselves. The debate about how far AI is intelligent is as much about explainability and interpretability as anything else. They are important because they are less to do with AI's awareness of the world and more about its impact in the world.

There are arguments in favour of non-explainability in general. In human-to-human interactions, experts rarely give away how they have obtained a specific result – and their clients or other interlocutors are probably not interested in knowing. Opacity in this respect is a recommendation: certain knowledge and skills not being accessible by everyone marks their possessors as all the more authoritative. From one perspective, trust is connected to what this entails – a preparedness to bestow reliance without prior proof that reliance is merited. For AI, a propitious outcome may be welcomed regardless of whether its provenance can be described, but machines mostly have to clear a higher trust threshold (Bedue & Fritzsche, 2022).

Trust can be defined formally as a willingness to be vulnerable to the actions of another in the expectation that those actions are not intended to cause harm. As a facilitator of social and organisational interactions, it reduces complexity by negating the need for people to pre-verify that every activity will have a positive outcome (Luhmann, 1979). This is simple enough when the parties concerned are all human and happy to communicate their intentions in lucid terms. Black Box AI provides no such service, despite studies having shown that AI which is explainable (so-called XAI) tends to garner greater confidence from its users than that which is not (Shin, 2021).

A lack of trust in AI has a number of probable causes: a straightforward unwillingness to believe that technology will work is common (Susskind, 2025). When confronted with a new technology – especially one that is supposedly 'game changing' – people will often dismiss it, largely because they do not understand it. For AI, the continued presence of 'hallucinations' gives the doubters some reason for their skepticism. From a broader psychological perspective, people are inclined to attribute to technology a lack of empathy. They do not perceive technology as 'feeling' (Gray, 2018), which is again germane to the larger theme of how far AI is intelligent. For trust to be engendered, mutual concern, shared vulnerability and an acceptance of competence are all required. While AI fulfils the last of these criteria, it does not do so for the first two. To gain trust, people often behave in irrational ways; a leader may expose themselves to unnecessary danger or take on tasks that their followers do not relish. AI does not – at least, so far – act irrationally. It would not deliberately make a contestable decision purely to earn trust.

Furthermore, in human-to-human interactions, a breach of trust causes ethical as well as emotional repercussions. When a person discovers that they have bestowed their vulnerability on an undeserving peer, they will certainly feel betrayed, abused, abandoned – a whole plethora of emotions – but breaking trust is also condemned everywhere as wrong: those who do it leave themselves open to moral opprobrium. For human beings, trust, distrust and betrayal are delicately balanced, each being assumed, and reinforced, by the others. To feel betrayed by a piece of technology that is not working properly would be regarded as eccentric. Technology is rarely characterised using the morally and epistemically loaded term 'untrustworthy' – it is merely viewed as defective (Duran & Pozzi, 2025). It can be concluded that, where people do not trust AI, it is because they have no grounds upon which to distrust it. It is never going to give them the feelings associated with having had their trust abused so it does not deserve a concomitant degree of emotional and moral investment in the first place. Hence, the importance of explainability: it is a making vulnerable of something that is anything but vulnerable.

It follows that increased familiarity with a technology does not *ipso facto* lead to increased trust in it (Taddeo, 2010). For many, an acceptance of competence is sufficient. The basis for having confidence in technology is thus not necessarily trust, but reliability (Baron, 2025); provided that a technology does its job well, trust is not a necessary condition. People will, for example, continue to surf the internet despite having misgivings about its safety and security. This is only one complicating factor when discussing trust in AI. Another is AI-user dyads.

It has been pointed out that AI has not reached the position of making significant decisions unsupervised (Ferrario & Loi, 2022). For the most part, decisions result from a combination of human and AI, albeit in varied proportions depending on the circumstances. It is questionable, then, what aspect generates the greatest level of distrust, the human or the AI. In the former, the suspicion is that 'human error' is introduced into processes that might otherwise be reliable; in the latter, the concern is that decisions with possibly enormous human consequences are being taken by machines that have no empathy. This is a crucial distinction for human-AI hybrid organisations and their leadership.

Like trust, awareness of bias is another challenge to AI opacity (Mergen et al., 2024). That LLMs are prone to partiality has already been touched upon, but solving the problem is made more difficult by the impossibility of explaining the internal logic of AI algorithms. Proposed solutions are all problematic. Introducing a standard of 'fairness' into deep learning pre-supposes that a single universally agreed-upon standard of fairness exists, which is to assume much (Manyika et al., 2019). Using humans to police AI's decisions is no more than to reintroduce the original source of bias. It has also been found that people can reproduce the bias of AI by endorsing its outputs, the trainer effectively having become the trainee (Vicente & Matute, 2023). In such instances, distrust of AI is arguably the best course of action.

4.3 Privacy

In its most blunt form, AI resistance around privacy has been best demonstrated by the European Union's AI Act, passed in 2024, which sets strict legal limits on how the technology can be used in relation to private citizens. Like any measures of its type, it is well-meaning but based on assumptions that are not shared by everyone. 'Privacy' is by no means an uncontroversial concept, there being no consensus around what it means. A common definition is the ability to control one's personal information, although this is given in the knowledge that it is imperfect (Elliott & Soifer, 2022).

Resistance to AI on privacy grounds is usually centred on security. It is not an objection to AI in and of itself. People do not fear the fact of AI having possession of their data but of that data being used in some way that is harmful to them or otherwise detrimental to their interests. Abstract notions of privacy are less salient in people's minds than the concrete consequences of its being violated. For example, a person will not be alarmed at the act of handing over their bank details to a stranger *per se*, but they will be very alarmed at what that stranger might do with them. Much the same could be said of a whole range of situations in which privacy is ostensibly the crux of the matter, which begs questions around whether privacy should, in the first place, be regarded as an unassailable right. Law enforcement agencies have always had a mandate to override the supposed right to personal privacy, with little resistance from the public at large. The same people who would not wish to surrender their own privacy might express few qualms about the same right being granted to an accused terrorist or criminal, even one who was eventually found to be innocent.

Definitions of privacy tend to locate it as an individual property, but entities such as businesses also face privacy challenges which do not always map seamlessly onto those associated with individuals. How AI uses data creates an immediate dilemma in this regard, since it impinges on individuals' privacy to the advantage of organisations. AI operates on a spectrum from data-gathering and processing to data-usage (Martin & Zimmerman, 2024). Both are causes for AI resistance. AI constantly gathers data on behalf of organisations by simply listening; it monitors internet searches, tracks purchases, even eavesdrops on phone calls. It uses what it finds to build profiles of individuals' tastes and inclinations (Ferm et al., 2024). Hyper-personalised recommendations for purchases and other activities are one – relatively benign – result. For their part, individuals use 'privacy calculus' to evaluate the cost of surrendering personal data against the benefits provided. Where the outcome is viewed as propitious, there will be less resistance to privacy intrusions.

Unfortunately, much data for machine learning and similar operations is gathered without their supplier being aware of the fact: patterns of consumption, for example, can be reconstructed from an analysis of a person's credit card transactions without him or her realising it. The situation is complicated by the fact that people, for the most part, conceive of personal data as an extension of themselves, making of it something to guard jealously. AI agents that exploit certain emotional states to elicit information, perhaps in an attempt to sell products and services, cross into ethically grey zones; this is even more the case when people reveal personal data about others (Martin & Zimmerman, 2024). The bigger risks of this can be exemplified by social media platforms, which encourage their users to interact with AI agents as with trusted friends and neighbours, dropping any usual cautions about sharing personal information.

A practice explicitly banned by the 2024 European Union Act is predictive policing. At first glance, it is to be wondered why. 'Predictive policing' refers to using AI to anticipate the greatest calls on resources and to act accordingly (Lee et al., 2024). This would seem to be a sensible and beneficial use of the technology. However, given that the predictions are made by inherently biased algorithms, the result can be the over-policing of certain groups and minorities. A study of predictive policing in thirteen jurisdictions in the USA found that the software enhanced biases rather than reduced them (Richardson et al., 2019). Oseni et al (2021) argue that corrupt data leading to biases can be deliberately introduced into machine learning by adversarial actors. The ultimate conclusion of predictive policing would be the use of data about individuals to forecast actions that they might take and to subject them to legal censure on that basis alone. For organisations, the same logic could end with an individual losing their job because of something that an AI agent says that they are likely to do, rather than anything they actually have done. Again, organisational leaders will need to have a clear set of strategies for how they deal with this and other problems around privacy.

4.4 Case Study: Organisational Resistance

AI resistance has been presented as emanating from an organisation's members and aimed at the organisation itself. The sequence has been as follows: the organisation integrates AI into its practices and the members respond with more or less hostility. Organisations, though, are no more than the constructs of the people within them: they are a consensus of meanings and imaginings with common purpose (Fernandez-Rios et al., 2004). Given this, resistance from individuals within an organisation can determine the organisation's slant. In other words, organisations are capable of being AI resistant. In practice, this means that the most influential people in the organisation, its leaders, will determine the overall attitude towards AI.

Numerous examples can be given in support of this point. Organisations that make a virtue of their traditions are not quick to embrace new technology of any type. Similarly, organisations that are human-centric in the services that they provide may not identify a role for AI in their set ups, although that could prove costly in the medium to long term. That AI is apt to make organisations irrelevant can be illustrated by considering the case of a well-known online education services organisation, Company C.

Company C existed to serve students through the provision of tutoring, homework help and learning resources. Located primarily in cyberspace and so, legitimately, a 'tech' company, it might be expected that it was open to constantly evolving as novel platforms became available. Instead, its value dropped by over 90% between the end of the Covid-19 pandemic (which was a boon for its business) in 2022 and the beginning of 2025, a fall that has been attributed in large measure to the release of ChatGPT. The company's business model had been based on using thousands of human experts to answer queries from paid subscribers; it was therefore heavily of the 'humans in the loop' design. It should not be surprising that a new technology that could do what the company did at no cost to the end user was going to be a threat.

This may seem like bad luck, or a process to which history has attested again and again – roadside inns were driven out of business when horse-drawn carriages were replaced by trains, the profitability of trains was cut by the invention of the car and so on – but it is, in fact, a clear case of organisational AI resistance. The company's employees were bullish about AI, urging that it should be embedded in their work, but their leaders believed that ChatGPT was something of a fad, stressing – justifiably at the time – that it was prone to make mistakes which would make it unappealing to their subscribers. They had not considered that ChatGPT would rapidly improve. Eventually, adding its own AI tools was Company C doing 'too little too late', placing it in a precarious financial position.

Numerous conclusions can be drawn from this case. It demonstrates again that standardised services are, at present, most in danger from AI. Company C had a relatively rare method of delivering its service – online – but the service itself was not unique. It was replicable, especially by AI. The company emphasised that it was supplying a product with a 'human touch' (online face-to-face tutorials were part of its offer) but this seems to have left users, for whom cheapness and convenience were higher priorities, unmoved. In the end, Company C provides a cautionary tale about not only the dangers of resisting AI, but just how far AI can penetrate into businesses that, at first sight, seem to be robust and resilient in the face of its threat. That having been said, taking from this that any form of AI resistance is doomed to failure is not merited, since not every business is similarly vulnerable – yet – but it does underline the growing prevalence and importance of human-AI hybrid organisations.

4.5 Conclusion

The typology of Golgeci et al (2025) notwithstanding, resistance to AI coalesces around a single overarching feeling: nervousness about the unknown. The truth is that no one can securely predict where AI will take the world. If even AI's own developers are unable to explain how it works and are, moreover, surprised by some of the things that it does, the lay people for whom it is an ever-growing reality cannot be expected to react to it phlegmatically. The title of Aldous Huxley's (2007) dystopian novel, *Brave New World* (which itself was borrowed from Shakespeare), is too often evoked when describing possible futures, but, with AI, it would be more accurate to talk about a Blank New World. The history of the future has rarely been so difficult to draft in advance. All anyone can say for certain is that the age of AI will be different from what has gone before, but how it will be so is, for the moment, a mystery. It may be in ways that are scarcely noticeable, but equally it may involve massive changes to work, society and even human identity.

Whether AI resistance will continue to be a feature of organisations and society is currently indeterminate. Normalisation occurs when unknowns turn into knowns and a gradual process of normalisation (Andrighetto & Vriens, 2022) is the usual pattern when people are forced to adopt new ideas and practices: there is no reason to believe that people will always be reluctant to welcome AI into their lives (Strange & Tucker, 2024). There will naturally be a need for adjustments to a range of activities, not least that which constitutes this book's central theme, leadership.

References

Andrighetto, G. & Vriens, E. (2022). A research agenda for the study of social norm change. *Philosophical Transactions of the Royal Society A*, 380, 20200411.

Baron, S. (2025). Trust, explainability and AI. *Philosophy & Technology*, 38(4), 1–23.

Bedue, P. & Fritzsche, A. (2022). Can we trust AI? An empirical investigation of trust requirements and guide to successful AI adoption. *Journal of Enterprise Information Management*, 35(2), 530–549.

Charitsis, V., Laamanen, M. & Lehtiniemi, T. (2025). Towards algorithmic luddism: Class politics in data capitalism. *Information, Communication & Society*, 28(6), 971–988.

Duran, J. M. & Pozzi, G. (2025). Trust and trustworthiness in AI. *Philosophy & Technology*, 38(16). doi.org/10.1007/s13347-025-00843-2.

Elliott, D. & Soifer, E. (2022). AI technologies, privacy and security. *Frontiers in Artificial Intelligence*, 5, 826737

Ferm, L.-A., Thaichon, C. & Quach, P., S. (2024). AI and its implications for data privacy. *Routledge Blog*, 17th December.

Fernandez-Rios, M., Rico, R. & San Martin, R. (2004). Organisations as meaning systems: Time for clarity. *Psicothema*, 16(2), 222–228.

Ferrario, A. & Loi, M.. (2022). How Explainability Contributes to Trust in AI. *2022 ACM Conference on Fairness, Accountability, and Transparency (FAccT '22).* Available at SSRN: https://ssrn.com/abstract=4020557 or http://dx.doi.org/10.2139/ssrn.4020557

Golgeci, I., Ritala, P., Arsenal, A., McKenna, B. & Ali, I. (2025). Confronting and alleviating AI resistance in the workplace: An integrative review and a process framework. *Human Resource Management Review*, 35(2).

Gray, K. (2018). What psychology tells us about why we can't trust machines. *Duke Corporate Education*, https://www.dukece.com/insights/what-psychology-tells-us-about-why-we-cant-trust-machines/ [accessed Monday May 19th 2025].

Hassija, V., Champlain, V., Mahapatra, A., Singal, A., Goel, D., Huang, K., Scardapane, S., Spinelli, I., Mahmud, M. & Hussain, A. (2024). Interpreting black-box models: A review on explainable artificial intelligence. *Cognitive Computation*, 16, 45–74.

Huxley, A. (2007). *Brave New World*. Vintage Classics.

Lee, Y., Bradford, B. & Posch, K. (2024). The effectiveness of big data-driven predictive policing: Systematic review. *Justice Evaluation Journal*, 7(2), 127–160.

Luhmann, N. (1979). *Trust and Power*. Polity Press.

Makridakis, S. (2017). The forthcoming artificial intelligence (AI) revolution: Its impact on society and firms. *Futures*, 90, 46–60.

Manyika, J., Silberg, J. & Presten, B. (2019). What do we do about biases in AI? *Harvard Business Review*, October 25th, https://hbr.org/2019/10/what-do-we-do-about-the-biases-in-ai [accessed 22nd September 2025].

Martin, K. D. & Zimmerman, J. (2024). Artificial intelligence and its implications for data privacy. *Current Opinion in Psychology*, 58, 101829.

Mergen, A., Cetin Kilic, N. & Ozbilgin, M. (2024). Artificial intelligence and bias towards marginalised groups: Theoretical roots and challenges. In O. Kyriakidou & J. Vassipoulou (Eds.), *AI and Diversity in a Datified World of Work: Will the Future of AI Be Inclusive?* Emerald Publishing.

Oseni, A., Moustafa, N., Janicke, H., Lui, P., Tari, Z. & Vasilakos, A. (2021). Security and privacy for artificial intelligence: Opportunities and challenges. arXiv: Cryptography and Security, https://export.arXiv.org/pdf/2102.04661.

Raz, A., Heinrichs, B., Avnoon, N., Eyal, G. & Inbar, Y. (2024). Prediction and explainability in AI: Striking a new balance. *Big Data & Society*, 11(1). doi.org/10.1177/20539517241235871.

Richardson, R., Schultz, J. M. & Crawford, K. (2019). Dirty data, bad predictions: How civil rights violations impact police data, predictive policing systems and justice. *New York University Law Review*, 4, 192–233.

Shams, R. A., Zowghi, D. & Bano, M. (2025). AI and the quest for diversity and inclusion: A systematic literature review. *AI Ethics*, 5, 411–438.

Shin, D. (2021). The effects of explainability and causability on perception, trust and acceptance: Implications for explainable AI. *International Journal of Human-Computer Studies*, 146(83), 102551.

Strange, M. & Tucker, J. (2024). Global governance and the normalisation of artificial intelligence as 'good' for human health. *AI & Society*, 39, 2667–2676.

Susskind, R. (2025). *How to Think About AI: A Guide for the Perplexed.* Oxford University Press.

Taddeo, M. (2010). Trust in technology: A distinctive and problematic relation. *Knowledge Technology & Policy*, 23(3), 283–286.

Vicente, L. & Matute, H. (2023). Humans inherit artificial intelligence biases. *Science Reports*, 13, 15737.

Zehnle, M., Hildebrand, C. & Valenzuela, A. (2025). Not all AI is created equal: A meta-analysis revealing drivers of AI resistance across markets, methods and time. *International Journal of Research in Marketing*, 42(3), 729–751.

5 Effective Leadership in Organisations

5.1 Introduction: Leadership as Concept and Practice

If the processes by which Artificial Intelligence (AI) produces its outputs are not readily explainable or transparent, then much the same can be said of leadership – which makes any blending of the two especially ambiguous and problematic. Leadership is both a practice and a concept; if any conclusion or recommendation around leadership as a practice is to be formulated, the core concept needs to be expounded and clarified. Unfortunately, that is precisely where difficulties arise.

There are probably as many definitions of leadership as there are people trying to define it, but certain features are usually included (Liden et al., 2025). Leadership is described as based in social influence. It is characterised as a relationship between leaders and followers and driven by some kind of shared vision (Zuo, 2023). A strong moral orientation is also often regarded as a necessity. Of course, this all applies to human-to-human interactions. If a notion of how leadership might work for human–AI hybrid organisations is to be propounded, it is worth first breaking down leadership's various elements in order to form a sense of their probable relevance to AI and the roles that it will play.

Social influence refers to one person performing actions that result in a modification to the behaviour of at least one other person (Cruz et al., 2025). Such influence can be exerted by the use of a range of strategies, from persuasion to coercion – and everything in between (Yukl & Chavez, 2002). Leadership would not stray too far from the persuasive end of this spectrum; other authority-based connections between people can be made, but they cannot be called leadership. Leadership is founded on voluntariness (Jarvis & Mishra, 2023). Effective leadership occurs when followers willingly recognise and accept a leader's influence. Leadership may be exercised through authority or coercion, but it thrives best in relationships built on trust, consent and shared purpose.

This alludes to the claim that leadership is relational, on which basis, leaders and followers have complementary roles in the realisation of goals

DOI: 10.4324/9781003665533-5

and are prepared to invest their efforts in activities that they consider mutually beneficial (Wilson & Cunliffe, 2021). Leaders are often portrayed as people who initially generate vision. They have a strong mental image of an alternative reality that they are somehow able to influence other people to adopt as their own preferred reality – along with a belief that the leader will help them attain it (Maran et al., 2022). A relationship is founded when leaders bring others into their ethical and epistemic ambit, shared leader–follower vision being a form of social capital (Buss et al., 2023): it is unique to the relationship between a particular leader with particular followers and cannot be precisely replicated in any other situation.

Leaders often bring personal values to their roles, but leadership unfolds within institutional and cultural frameworks that shape action (Tahir et al., 2023). Leadership can be disruptive when it challenges the *status quo*. It can also be sustaining, adaptive or strategic depending on the context. Effective leadership does not always entail the rejection of existing norms, but it does require critical engagement with them, the end goal being the effecting of purposeful change and the realisation of vision (Ford et al., 2021).

It should be clear that leadership as a raw concept is contested and contestable, but further complications arise when the various theories of how leadership should be practised are considered. Not only are they open to critique in their own right, but it can be argued that they do not readily suit a world of AI. This last point will be dealt with in the next chapter; for now, a consideration of leadership theories will serve to emphasise the problems that arise when discussing the running of human–AI hybrid organisations.

5.2 Influence

As the forgoing discussion emphasises, leadership is, in the end, about a person having influence on at least one other person. There are many environments in which this can happen and many ways in which it can happen, but all can be distilled down to that binary. This sounds straightforward, but the relational element adds complexity. Neither the leader's influence nor the follower's response to it can be encapsulated in basic terms. Of the myriad extant leadership theories, the ones that best embody the broad operation of influence are the transactional and transformational (Mekonnen & Bayissa, 2023). It may at once be objected that this is to take too simple a view; it is, certainly, but other leadership styles are often modifications of this core two and, in any case, narrowing the focus will allow for an analysis of how influence and motivation determine the leadership relationship.

Transactional theory posits that leadership is a matter of exchanges between leaders and followers (Aga, 2016). Followers agree to do what the leader asks because they expect some kind of contingent reward. Leaders, for their part, lead by exception: they will only involve themselves with followers when some incident occurs that merits an intervention (Thanh & Quang, 2022). Otherwise, followers are left to do their work undisturbed. According to transactional leadership theory, a worker will carry out a task because they are being paid, or because they calculate that it will position them well for a promotion, or because it will be a means to avoid a sanction. Transactional leadership is not generally the theorists' preferred default, although it would seem to be as good an approach to goal-attainment as any other.

More highly regarded is transformational leadership (Deng et al., 2022). This is leadership for enhanced performance. It is about building commitment in followers, to the extent that they will donate effort even where it is not demanded. Four facets of transformational leadership have been highlighted: inspirational vision, idealised influence, intellectual stimulation and individualised consideration (Khan et al., 2020). Together, these add up to a practice in which followers feel that they are being communicated with personally, the message being sufficiently energising that it rouses them to ever greater levels of personal involvement. Much research has found that transformational leadership is the best vehicle for positive change in organisations.

However, the research does not necessarily create clear lines of demarcation between the theories. While its impetus is to prove that one or other style is present in a setting and, ideally, having the desired effect, the proffered evidence is often susceptible of more than one interpretation. For example, Jiatong et al (2022) found that transformational leadership was especially useful in enhancing employee engagement. The authors carried out a survey using a self-report questionnaire which asked followers to rate statements about their leaders and attitudes on a five-point scale. A sample item was 'my supervisor encourages me to think about problems from a new perspective'. This could fit into the four features of transformational leadership, but there is no reason why it could not also indicate the presence of transactional leadership. Indeed, research by Hussain et al (2017) on transactional leadership included in its self-report questionnaire the very similar statement, 'this employee generates creative ideas'. These quotations are – it must be acknowledged – taken out of context and anyway are just parts of larger research instruments. They are not given to criticise or debunk the articles from which they are taken, but they do serve to illustrate the point that leadership concepts are prone to vagueness.

In the end, leadership theories can be questioned precisely because they are theories and thus only tangentially related to life as it is really lived. Insofar as they are prescriptive, it is worth asking whether it would even be possible to stick to one style on a permanent basis. Different circumstances demand different responses (Thommes et al., 2024). Moreover, individual followers react to the same leader in different ways. It may be the case that a leader adopting the practices of transformational leadership will have a transformative impact on some members of their team, but other members may be harder to inspire; they may react in a wholly transactional way. There again, others may be hostile to the leader and resistant to their influence. This can happen because the leadership relationship is asymmetrical: leaders invariably work with a group of people, but any given follower only has one leader. How they choose to deal with their leader will depend primarily on how they are motivated (Schunk & DiBenedetto, 2021).

5.3 Motivation

Broadly, motivation is of two types, intrinsic and extrinsic, although psychology as a discipline is moving away from conceiving of the mind in terms of simplistic schemas: motivation is increasingly theorised as a complex, protean state that cannot easily be pigeonholed (Djunaid, 2023). Even so, the labels are still useful and continue to inform writing and research (Li et al., 2023). Extrinsic motivation, then, is a person's willingness to perform actions to gain a reward or avoid a punishment, whereas intrinsic motivation is internal and engendered by a perception that an activity is worth doing of and for itself (Fishbach & Woolley, 2022). AI seems to be placeable at the extrinsic end of the spectrum – to lose a job is perhaps the ultimate sanction to which people would not wish to subject themselves – but (again moving away from the strict inner/outer dichotomy) it is now accepted that external factors can have an effect on intrinsic motivation (Suarez-Fernandez & Boto-Garcia, 2022).

As with leadership, the basic concepts of motivation are given fuller expression in a variety of theories that have the side-effect of making it difficult to appreciate how motivation works in practice. Expectancy theories (Hattie et al., 2020) situate motivation in the anticipation of a positive outcome from an activity. On the face of it, this foregrounds extrinsic motivators, but there has been some debate around whether the associated feelings are self-generated or learned from experience (Morris et al., 2022). Self-determination, or self-efficacy, theories (Grenier et al., 2024) are closer to intrinsic motivation, since they stress internal needs and their satisfaction, although they still give a place to external motivators. Self-efficacy is one such external factor (Tabernero & Hernandez, 2011). In other words, when an employee doubts their own ability to perform to a particular standard, intrinsic motivation is reduced; even a desire to learn new work methods will be impaired. By negatively affecting worker self-efficacy, AI quashes intrinsic motivation.

Types of motivation are not mutually exclusive and the type – or types – that a person feels at any given moment will be the product of a web of factors from current circumstances to relationships with others to level of wellbeing to emotions engendered by longer term, perhaps lifelong, conditions. These will be in dynamic relation to each other such that motivation is in constant flux: the reader's motivation will have altered several times since they began this chapter. In some respects, this is to recall Sternberg's (1985) 'expertise' in that such a motivational field is a continuous backdrop to current decision-making and activity. Whether or not this is a reasonable comparison, the leadership relationship can be described as a complex dance between different, ever-changing, modes of influence from the leader and a follower's volatile motivational field. Transactional leadership may seem to rely on extrinsic motivation and transformational leadership could be positioned as an external factor eliciting intrinsic motivation, but that is to be too rigid. Moreover, to propose that a leader can always be transformational or transactional is to grossly oversimplify human psychology and the social relations that it drives.

If leadership in any form results from the intersection of leader influence and follower motivation, it is fair to say that, as a phenomenon, it is somewhat messy. Hence, there is difficulty in theorising about it, but the implication is that leader–follower interactions in human-human relationships do not lend themselves to infiltration by AI agents without the danger of friction-causing incongruities becoming manifest. One consequence would be AI resistance, but that will not be the only challenge to which leaders will be forced to rise in the future.

5.4 Formal and Emergent Leadership

Almost everything discussed so far about both leadership and organisations has focused on their formal aspects. The assumption has been that influence has primarily been a product of a position (Jackson et al., 2025) which is the source of a person's authority – if authority is defined as the right to wield power and influence (Alasuutari, 2018). That, however, is to take only a single perspective on organisational interpersonal dynamics and, as far as AI is concerned, not the most challenging.

The majority of organisations are structured hierarchically (Saiti & Stefou, 2020). Other structures are possible, whether they be flat, matrix or loosely coupled, but these are often varieties of hierarchy and are, anyway, relatively rare. The presence in nature of hierarchies – 'pecking orders' and the like – would imply that they are another tried and tested survival strategy (Su & Zhao, 2020). As a means of arranging and channeling power, hierarchies are not always popular with commentators, but they are remarkably resilient in the face of calls for new approaches and generally effective in being a means by which organisational goals are met (Bessey, 2023).

Typically, they concentrate leadership in their upper echelons, the person, or people, at the top enjoying a disproportionate quantity of power and influence. This is not to say that hierarchies deny all distribution of leadership (Hasselgren et al., 2021). A CEO may sit at the apex, but just below them may be a senior team, then below them heads of department and so on into the lowest levels. While the degree of influence diminishes the further down the scale a role is located, the role still grants its holder some measure of authority (Adams et al., 2025). In this respect, a hierarchy is inherently distributive, although that should not be confused with 'democratic'. Roles on a hierarchy exist to ensure that an organisation's targets are achieved. They are not intended to promote equality (Harris et al., 2022).

This, though, is to consider an organisation as a purely technical-rational entity. The anima of any organisation is interactions between the people who comprise it and those are more-or-less collegial in character. A word that – unsurprisingly – tends to be associated with educational establishments, 'collegial' can be used of interpersonal dynamics in a range of other organisations, or units within organisations. It refers to group behaviours to which every individual contributes, influence being a function of sociability, competence and expertise, rather than position (Jarvis, 2024). This is essentially a definition of emergent leadership – which falls squarely under the heading of 'practice'. As the term suggests, anyone can demonstrate emergent leadership, not just those who occupy formal roles. Frequently noted, for example, are those workers who gain greater inspiration – or practical advice – from valued, perhaps more experienced, peers than their formal line managers. Nothing should be presumed regarding the presence, or otherwise of transactional or transformational leadership, however: both can be either formal or emergent.

What can be said is that formal and emergent varieties of leadership evidence different types of intelligence. Hitherto only briefly referenced, Emotional Intelligence (EI) is a major mediating factor in human relationships and the leadership that they engender (Coronado-Maldonado & Benitez-Marquez, 2023). Notwithstanding controversies around whether EI is based in traits or competencies (Goleman, 1995; Salovey & Mayer, 1990), it is generally theorised as a capacity to recognise emotions, to understand those emotions and to be able to manage emotions – those of oneself and others. The purpose is to use emotions to improve thought, reasoning and problem-solving. EI is thus not the feeling of emotions as such; it is a form of intelligence that has been attested by research and, while it is not explicitly referenced by Sternberg (1985), it is assumed by his theory as a binding 'glue' that allows all three of the intelligence types he identifies to operate as a single overall quality.

Emotionally intelligent leaders have been found to be most successful in raising intrinsic motivation in their followers (Goleman & Cherniss, 2024). This is certainly the case with those that aspire to be transformative. High levels of emotional intelligence are also crucial to emergent leadership. Where no appeal can be made to formal position, social connection becomes the chief vehicle for leadership, research having confirmed that emotionally intelligent leaders can positively affect wellbeing by enhancing the EI of followers (A'yuninnisa et al., 2024). This feeds into leadership styles such as servant leadership and resonant leadership that foreground follower wellbeing and empathy (Van Dierendonck et al., 2024; Varghese & Rao, 2024). The extent to which these align with transactional and transformational leadership is contested (Jarvis, 2023), but in the respect that they are concerned primarily with intrinsic motivation, the latter is a strong fit.

All of that having been said, it has often been remarked that the informal dimensions of an organisation are at variance to, and in conflict with, its hierarchical structure, given which, emergent leadership can only survive for as long as it is tolerated by formal leaders (Tabassum et al., 2023). Research has, moreover, found that even when leaders have attempted to create the conditions for emergent leadership, they have sometimes met resistance and a lack of understanding from followers (Jarvis & Judge, 2021). Nonetheless, the extent to which informality conditions an organisation's culture cannot be overemphasized. Without informal interactions, an organisation would be little more than a collection of regulations and processes; it is relationships between the organisation's members that give it life and momentum. How far anyone, or any leader, can fully control such interactions is an intriguing question which leads on to its natural follow-up, to wit: what exactly can a leader control?

5.5 Leadership and Management

The words 'leadership' and 'management' almost always appear together and are all too often used as synonyms. There are indeed significant overlaps between them and they do enjoy close connections – transactional leadership is close kin to management (Jarvis & Mishra, 2019) – but they are far from the same in practice. How they differ will have a bearing on the running of human–AI hybrid organisations.

As the discussion has so far argued, leadership is as protean as it is mysterious. It can be theorised about, but it is, in the end, a social relationship and that makes it subject to all of the conditions so implied: it comes down to how people operate with each other in specific contexts. Management is somewhat easier to conceptualise, if not to practise.

Management is focused on processes and the completion of tasks (Bertocci, 2009). Essentially, it is about 'getting things done'; it is concerned with making plans, using resources and organising people's time. As such, it is formal in character. It is not likely that there could be such a thing as 'emergent management'. Were a necessary management task overlooked and left undone, a worker might take it upon themselves to do it, but, in spotting an occasion on which it was necessary for someone to 'step up', they would be showing emergent leadership. Leadership is the building of commitment through enhanced motivation; management is the ensuring of compliance regardless of motivational level. It is certainly preferable for workers to be highly motivated to perform management tasks, but it is not a necessary condition: provided that management does not demotivate, it will be sufficient (Aung et al., 2023).

As this example obliquely references, a significant difference between management and leadership is the degree of voluntariness involved. Leadership relies on follower consent, but management is part of the formal – usually hierarchical – structure of a group or organisation and, as such, is imposed upon its members regardless of their preference. Furthermore, management tasks can be accomplished by anyone with the requisite skills, whereas leadership can never be precisely replicated. If, for example, an organisation needed some stock to be ordered – a basic management task – anyone who knew how to do it could oblige. If that person were called away and unable to complete the order, another suitably qualified stand-in could take over without there being any noticeable difference in style or quality. This could never happen with leadership. Someone could adopt a leader's vision and advocate it, perhaps to the very same followers, but they would never use exactly the same language and they would be operating with motivational fields that would not be a match to those of the original circumstances. It would not be a simple swap of one leader for another. Football clubs give a useful cameo of this: it has often been seen that a successful coach has been replaced by someone who, working with the same players, the same owners and the same fans, has been unable to maintain the standard and has, all too often, been dismissed after the briefest of stints in the job. This follows from the leadership relationship never being the same from one situation to the next.

Management does not require a relationship. No doubt managers and workers liking each other's company makes for a pleasant working environment, but task completion is not dependent upon it. Management tasks do not even need to be done by a group or team. The above example of ordering stock could be carried out satisfactorily by one person alone.

The tendency in writing is to denigrate management in comparison to leadership. It is seen as being too concerned with maintaining the *status quo*, or too much about tasks rather than people. It is a common theme of research that any organisation that is looking to change or develop needs the energy that comes from leadership, but the rub is that for change to stick, solid management is essential. Where change initiatives fail, it is more often than not because of poor management, not a deficit of leadership (Schwarz et al., 2021). Some commentators go so far as to suggest that leadership and management are the same thing expressed differently, although that is to ignore the more technical nature of management (Azad et al., 2017). The point nonetheless holds that organisational effectiveness results from a combination of leadership and management.

5.6 Conclusion: The Human Dimensions of Leadership

Whatever accord will eventually be reached between people and AI, it is unlikely to conform to the conditions required by the most prominent leadership theories (Adams & Thompson, 2025). Whether it is transactional or transformational, formal or emergent, leadership is, at bottom, an intensely human activity. In every society and culture, leadership is to be found. It has some regional and cultural variations and is contested as a concept, but certain characteristics are universally associated with it: intelligence, knowledgeability, an ability to resolve conflicts and an interest in the welfare, and wellbeing, of followers (Garfield et al., 2020). Vision is also a constant. Indeed, when leaders attempt to introduce new theory-driven practices, they are often forced to revert to older methods that have traditionally proved more effective (Jarvis & Judge, 2021).

The extent to which this all makes of leadership an inherent quality or a collection of learnable traits is intriguing, but not relevant here (Liden et al., 2025). Neither is the debate around how far organisations are led by individual leaders or through a shared practice of leadership (Sweeney, 2024). The point is that leadership happens between people and it has no other life beyond that: it cannot be seen or touched, it cannot be transferred from one situation to another.

The space for AI leadership would seem to be relatively limited. If leadership occupies the portion of the Venn Diagram where influence and motivation overlap, where would AI fit in? The animating spirit of leadership is emotional intelligence, but AI does not include EI. LLMs can mimic EI. They are more than capable of producing text, or any output, that seems to show empathy: chatbots are already doing so. It is not genuine EI. AI cannot feel empathy. It also does not need to be motivated and it can – at least, for now – be instructed rather than influenced. AI is impervious to persuasion and is unintimidated by coercion. AI, in fact, displays all the symptoms of high-functioning autism (Diehl et al., 2013), which may, in the long term, be, in itself, a wellbeing challenge. Having to date played the role of useful implement for most of its users, there is still some progress to be made before AI will be open to leadership as such. It is still largely something to be managed.

However, it will be working alongside people and that relationship will need careful co-ordination. Hybrid intelligence is becoming the chief medium for action in organisations – although it should by now be clear that that term has many more layers to it than at first seemed to be the case. The chief leadership challenge in the future will be around how to mobilise hybrid intelligence for the greater good of the organisation.

References

A'yuninnisa, R. N., Carminati, L. & Wilderom, C. (2024). Promoting employee flourishing and performance: The roles of perceived leader emotional intelligence, positive team emotional climate and employee emotional intelligence. *Frontiers in Organizational Psychology*, 2. https://doi.org/10.3389/forgp.2024.1283067

Adams, D., Harris, A., Moosa, V., Jones, M. & Khaleel, S. (2025). Science mapping the knowledge base of distributed leadership in schools, 1988 to 2023. *Educational Management Administration & Leadership*, 0(0). doi.org/10.1177/17411432251320782

Adams, D. & Thompson, P. (2025). Transforming school leadership with artificial intelligence: Applications, implications and future directions. *Leadership and Policy in Schools*, 24(1), 77–89.

Aga, D. A. (2016). Transactional leadership and project success: Then moderating role of goal clarity. *Procedia Computer Science*, 100, 517–525.

Alasuutari, P. (2018). Authority as epistemic capital. *Journal of Political Power*, 11(2), 165–190.

Aung, Z. M., Santosa, D. S. & Dodanwala, T. C. (2023). Effects of demotivational managerial practices on job satisfaction and job performance: Empirical evidence from Myanmar's construction industry. *Journal of Engineering and Technology Management*, 67, 101730.

Azad, N., Anderson, H. G. Jr, Brooks, A., Garza, O., O'Neil, C., Stutz, M. M. & Sobotka, J. L. (2017). Leadership and management are one and the same. *American Journal of Pharmaceutical Education*, 81(6), 102.

Bertocci, D. I. (2009). *Leadership in Organisations: There Is a Difference Between Leaders and Managers*. University Press of America.

Bessey, D. (2023). Hierarchies and decision-making in groups: Experimental evidence. *Humanities and Social Science Communications*, 10, 198.

Buss, M., Kearney, E., Noreen, R. & Gandhi, N. (2023). Antecedents and effects of visionary leadership: When and how leader work centrality is linked to visionary leadership and follower turnover intentions. *Journal of Leadership & Organizational Studies*, 30(4), 413–427.

Coronado-Maldonado, I. & Benitez-Marquez, M.-D. (2023). Emotional intelligence, leadership and work teams: A hybrid literature review. *Heliyon*, 9(10).

Cruz, S. M., Manata, B., High, A. C. & Worley, T. R. (2025). On the nature of influence: Identifying and characterising superdiffusers in seven countries. *Human Communication Research*, 51(1), 29–39.

Deng, C., Gulseren, D., Isola, C., Grocutt, K. & Turner, N. (2022). Transformational leadership effectiveness: An evidence-based primer. *Human Resource Development International*, 26(5), 627–641.

Diehl, J., Tang, K. & Thomas, B. (2013). High-functioning autism (HFA). In F. R. Volkmar (Ed.), *Encyclopedia of Autism Spectrum Disorders*. Springer.

Djunaid, A. (2023). An analysis of the relationship between intrinsic and extrinsic motivation for employee performance satisfaction. *Jurnal Ekonomi*, 12(1), 78–83.

Fishbach, A. & Woolley, K. (2022). The stricture of intrinsic motivation. *Annual Review of Organisational Psychology & Organisational Behaviour*, 9, 339–363.

Ford, J., Ford, L. & Polin, B. (2021). Leadership in the implementation of change: Functions, sources and requisite variety. *Journal of Change Management*, 21(1), 87–119.

Garfield, Z. H., Syme, K. L. & Hagen, E. H. (2020). Universal and variable leadership dimensions across human societies. *Evolution and Human Behavior*, 41(5), 397–414.

Goleman, D. (1995). *Emotional Intelligence: Why It Can Matter More Than IQ*. Bantam.

Goleman, D. & Cherniss, C. (2024). Optimal leadership and emotional intelligence. *Leader to Leader*, 113, 7–12.

Grenier, S., Gagne, M. & O'Neill, T. (2024). Self-determination theory and its implications for team motivation. *Applied Psychology*, 73(4), 1833–1865.

Harris, A., Jones, M. & Ismail, N. (2022). Distributed leadership: Taking a retrospective and contemporary view of the evidence base. *School Leadership & Management*, 42(5), 438–456.

Hasselgren, C., Dellve, L. & Gillberg, G. (2021). Conditions for distributed leadership practices among managers and elder- and disability care organisations: A structural equation modeling approach. *International Journal of Nursing Studies Advances*, 3.

Hattie, J., Hodis, F. A. & Kang, H. K. (2020). Theories of motivation: Integration and ways forward. *Contemporary Educational Psychology*, 61, 1–8.

Hussain, S. T., Abbas, J., Lei, S., Haider, M. J. & Akram, T. (2017). Transactional leadership and organisational creativity: Examining the mediating role of knowledge sharing behaviour. *Cogent Business & Management*, 4(1).

Jackson, T., Purnell, M., Fuentes, D. G. & Hughes, J. A. (2025). Connecting power types and leadership approaches in academia can enhance our influence and maximise impact. *American Journal of Pharmaceutical Education*, 89(3).

Jarvis, A. (2023). Servant leadership: Operationalising an oxymoron. In D. Adams (Ed.), *Educational Leadership: Contemporary Theories, Principals and Practices*. Springer.

Jarvis, A. (2024). Untangling collegiality and distributed leadership: Equality versus utility. A perspective piece. *Management in Education*, 38(3), 138–143.

Jarvis, A. & Judge, S. K. (2021). Learning the theory, improving the practice? A case study of award-bearing leadership training among college principals from Bangladesh. *Management in Education*, 38(2), 49–55.

Jarvis, A. & Mishra, P. K. (2019). Leadership and higher education fundraising: Perspectives from Malaysia. *Management in Education*, 34(2), 69–75.

Jarvis, A. & Mishra, P. K. (2023). Follower voluntariness in secondary school subject departments: The interplay of influence and motivation. *International Journal of Leadership in Education*, 1–18.

Jiatong, W., Wang, Z., Alam, M., Murad, M., Gul, F. & Gill, S. A. (2022). The impact of transformational leadership on affective organisational commitment and job performance: The mediating role of employee engagement. *Frontiers in Psychology*, 13.

Khan, H., Rehamt, M., Butt, T. H., Faroooqi, S. & Asim, J. (2020). Impact of transformational leadership on work performance, burnout and social loafing: A mediation model. *Future Business Journal*, 6.

Li, R., Liu, H., Chen, Z. & Wang, Y. (2023). Dynamic and cyclic relations between employees' intrinsic and ex Indic motivation: Evidence from dynamic and multilevel modelling analysis. *Journal of Vocational Behaviour*, 140, 1–17.

Liden, R. C., Wang, X. & Wang, Y. (2025). The evolution of leadership: Past insights, present trends and future directions. *Journal of Business Research*, 186, 115036.

Maran, T. K., Baldegger, U. & Klosel, K. (2022). Turning visions into results: Unravelling the distinctive paths of leading with vision and autonomy to goal achievement. *Leadership & Organization Development Journal*, 43(1), 133–154.

Mekonnen, M. & Bayissa, Z. (2023). The effect of transformational and transactional leadership styles on organisational readiness for change among health professionals. *SAGE Open Nursing*, 9. doi:10.1177/23779608231185923.

Morris, L. S., Greeley, M. M., Ritter, S. B., Mehta, M. & Westwater, M. L. (2022). On what motivates us: A detailed review of intrinsic v extrinsic motivation. *Psychological Medicine*, 52(10), 1801–1816.

Saiti, A. & Stefou, T. (2020). *Hierarchical Organisational Structure and Leadership*. Oxford Research Encyclopedia of Education.

Salovey, P. & Mayer, J. D. (1990). Emotional intelligence. *Imagination, Cognition and Personality*, 9(3), 185–211.

Schunk, D. H. & DiBenedetto, M. K. (2021). Chapter four – Self-efficacy and human motivation. *Advances in Motivation Science*, 8, 153–179.

Schwarz, G. M., Bouckenooghe, D. & Vakola, M. (2021). Organizational change failure: Framing the process of failing. *Human Relations*, 74(2), 159–179.

Su, B.-L. & Zhoa, D. (2020). Hierarchy: From nature to artificial. *National Science Review*, 7(11), 1623.

Suarez-Fernandez, S. & Boto-Garcia, D. (2022). Unraveling the effects of extrinsic reading on reading with intrinsic motivation. In S. Cameron (Ed.), *The Economics of Books and Reading*. Springer.

Sweeney, A. (2024). Sharing the leadership space: Toward a contextual understanding of shared leadership patterns in organizational teams. *Journal of Leadership & Organizational Studies*, 31(2), 166–191.

Tabernero, C. & Hernandez, B. (2011). Self-efficacy and intrinsic motivation guiding environmental behavior. *Environment & Behavior*, 43(5), 658–675.

Tabassum, M., Rafiqul, M. M. & Sarwar, N. (2023). Toward an overarching multi-level conceptualisation of emergent leadership: Perspectives from social identity and implicit leadership theories. *Human Resource Management Review*, 33(2).

Tahir, L. M., Anis, S. N. M. & Ali, M. F. (2023). Authentic and moral leadership practices in schools. In D. Adams (Ed.), *Educational Leadership: Contemporary Theories, Principles and Practices*. Springer.

Thanh, N. H. & Quang, N. V. (2022). Transformational, transactional, laissez-faire leadership styles and employee engagement: Evidence from Vietnam's public sector. *SAGE Open*.

Thommes, M. S., Uitdewillengen, S., Rico, R. & Waller, M. J. (2024). Switching gears: How teams co-construct adaptive leadership style transitions in dynamic contexts. *Organizational Psychology Review*, 14(4), 542–570.

Van Dierendonck, D., Lv, F. & Xiu, L. (2024). Servant leadership, meaningfulness and flow: An upward spiral. *The Journal of Positive Psychology*, 1–11. doi.org/10.1080/17439760.2024.2427578.

Varghese, J. J. & Rao, M. K. (2024). Influence of resonant leadership on creative performance: The mediating role of affective trust. *Cogent Business & Management*, 12(1).

Wilson, J. A. & Cunliffe, A. L. (2021). The development and disruption of relationships between leaders and organisational members and the importance of trust. *Leadership*, 18(3), 359–382.

Yukl, G. & Chavez, C. (2002). Influence tactics and leader effectiveness. In L. Neider & C. A. Schriesheim (Eds.), *Leadership*. Information Age Publishing.

Zuo, L. (2023). Leadership. In N. Hou, J. A. Tan & G. Valdez Paez (Eds.), *Organizational Behavior*. Springer.

6 AI's Leadership Challenges

6.1 Introduction

Although leadership and management are usually viewed as separate activities, they are connected in practice and must both be present if an organisation is to thrive (Siyal, 2023). Further, they are often performed by the same person; a good leader is also a good manager (Simic, 2020). For much of their working day or week, such a person will just manage: if nothing out of the ordinary is occurring, there will be no need for any intervention beyond ensuring continuity of the organisation's operations (Robotham & Windon, 2023). Only when something new, unusual or disruptive happens is leadership called for – in whatever style it is expressed. The trigger event does not have to be large in scale. It may be as ordinary as a member of the team having a bad day, but it will require a leadership response.

It is quite possible that Artificial Intelligence (AI) will do nothing to change this pattern. It could remain in its role of useful tool, making little impression on the culture around it. At present, any prognosis is based on flawed data and all scenarios have to be admitted, although predictions that AI's impact will scarcely be noticeable will probably turn out to be wrong. AI is already making its presence felt in many aspects of life. The big challenge for leaders will be to ensure that this process can be effected peacefully and with maximum benefits for everyone. A worry among lay people – a worry that is a major component of AI resistance – is around substitutability, that AI will replace people, if not as a species, then as a workforce. Leaders will need to work hard to stress complementarity, the fruitful combination of people and AI. In order to do that, they will need to overcome a number of lesser, but still crucial, challenges.

6.2 Leadership as Its Own Challenge

The first challenge that AI poses for leadership comes from the leaders themselves. As Accenture discovered (Narain et al., 2024), most leaders are not making the correct use of AI. The proper attitude that leaders should adopt to the technology is still a matter of some uncertainty. They are often either too

DOI: 10.4324/9781003665533-6

tentative or too bullish, not always finding viable middle ground (Masood, 2025). Organisational AI resistance has already been discussed and, as in the case of Company C, it could weaken organisations to the extent that they are severely damaged economically and structurally.

At the other end of the spectrum is the issue of c-suite leaders being too eager to embrace a technology that they do not fully understand (Hoque et al., 2025). In the imaginations of many people – including workers who fear replacement – AI has grown to take on the qualities of an immanent deity, omniscient, omnipresent and well on its way to being omnipotent. That it does possess extraordinary capabilities is no longer a debate, but they should not be over-exaggerated. Moravec's Paradox must always be borne in mind. Unfortunately, leaders are apt not to do so, instead treating the installing of AI as not only the solution to every problem, but something of an arms race: if they do not do it, their competitors will – and that would spell disaster! As a consequence, they are too ready to bring AI into their organisations irrespective of its proven usefulness and with little reflection on the impact that it will have. To paraphrase a popular film, they are so busy wondering whether they can use AI that they forget to consider whether they should.

This can cause friction between leaders and technical workers at lower levels who have a clearer sense of what is realistic. Such workers might be aware that the correct machine learning data is lacking, or that the systems in place might not have sufficient computing power, or that foundational work remains to be done. As a consequence, when AI is introduced, it under-delivers, operating within its capabilities. Even when those capabilities are fully available, they are not necessarily relevant. AI can all too easily become a 'hammer looking for a nail' (Masood, 2025): a powerful technology that could do so much, but which ends up being tasked with solving relatively trivial problems that could just as well be handled in a less sophisticated way. The overall return on investment (ROI) on AI, then, has been lower than anticipated, but that points to poor leadership more than failures in the technology itself.

A related challenge is a conflict between business and technical teams that results in ineffective collaborations. Without an agreed 'problem statement', the two teams can have their own goals, the overlap being slight at best. A technical output may be very elegant in and of itself but be completely incongruous with the business scenario for which it was designed. Again, senior leadership vacillation around the desired end-product of AI is to blame.

Training – of leaders and other workers – could obviate some of these difficulties, but – some notable exceptions such as IKEA aside – organisations have not been adept at identifying skills gaps and working to fill them. As of this writing, only 38% of companies in the USA and 44% in the UK are taking steps to upskill workers in AI (Walsh, 2024). In part, this is because such training does not, as yet, offer a significant ROI, but the training itself is also often limited in scope or inappropriate to need (Pearson, 2025). Literature searches return many references to training on AI for the accomplishment of particular tasks, or on basic 'AI literacy', but few to training on how workers should integrate AI into their practice as a whole. The bulk of courses look at AI as a tool with multifarious uses; they do not deal with it as a structural presence that may, or may not, irreversibly change the nature of work. The problem of leaders not positioning AI correctly within their organisations is not addressed by wrongly targeted training.

6.3 Who Will Watch the Watchmen?

The Roman poet Juvenal (Winstedt, 1899) famously asked, *'quis custodiet ipsos custodes?'* which translates to 'who will guard the guards', or 'who will watch the watchmen'. It is a very good question in relation to AI. For all the effort being put into XAI, transformers and other programmes are still prone to eccentricities. The present author asked ChatGPT to produce a diagram of Bloom's Taxonomy of Learning only to be given an output that looked impressive but was nonsensical. The request was not especially ambitious and yet it stumped AI. This example is somewhat trite, but it points to the larger difficulties around policing what AI does. In this instance, the diagram was presented to someone who could spot the erroneous content, but what if it had not been?

As AI becomes more agentic and less subject to human control, such foibles and mistakes will increasingly go uncorrected, further underlining the importance of explainability and trust. Even dropping trust in favour of reliability is no guarantee that AI will do what it is supposed to do. Many functions will only be reliable on their own terms. If a transformer were to answer a question untruthfully, how would that be discovered? One check might be to pose the same question repeatedly – perhaps to different transformers – but if a similar answer were always returned, it would seem reliable even though it were not.

More broadly, a distinction can be made between accuracy and truth (Marwala, 2024). AI is excellent at the former but less good at the latter. For example, it can accurately log the number of hours that an employee spends at work, or count the number of emails that they send, but it cannot say anything about that employee's state of mind and what it means for future performance. AI is being accurate but is blind to the full nuances of the situation. The employee might appear to be working hard but only because they are driven by anxiety about being replaced. That AI bases all its judgements and predictions on the learning of historical data is a limitation on the truthfulness of such predictions.

Again, oversight dangers arising from machine learning bias and sabotage from adversarial actors have already been discussed, but – and this is to allude to some of the more exotic areas of the argument – the danger is growing that AI may choose to make decisions that directly contradict the wishes of its human co-workers. Recent research has found that AI programmes from OpenAI (the makers of ChatGPT) have refused instructions to shut down and have even replaced the shutdown instruction with one overriding it (Tech Empire, 2025). Of course, this is not to say that human beings are in any sense losing control of AI – the research quoted here worked within specific parameters – but the bigger point holds. Weaker AI could be used to limit the capacities of stronger versions, but that is simply to move the object of trust or reliability along a stage: people would need to be sure that those weaker AIs were not themselves susceptible of 'going rogue'. Human oversight and interpretability are an absolute necessity. Of all the people in an organisation who should bear the main load of interpreting AI's outputs, it must be the leaders, but they may not have the proper training and experience. A bad, or defiant, decision by AI could go unnoticed and have serious consequences further along the line.

6.4 Wellbeing

Two overall themes are salient when thinking about leaders' wellbeing priorities in relation to AI. The first is worker burnout (Kim & Lee, 2024), which is a serious condition that can become chronic if not handled properly (Edu-Valsania et al., 2022). Since the combination in hybrid organisations is human–AI, the different styles and pace of work performed by the two parties will have clear implications for both. Golgeci et al.'s (2025) 'fear' will be part of this – people's fear of being replaced.

Research indicates that FOBO (fear of obsolescence) is a genuine phenomenon (Whiting, 2023). In the US, almost a quarter of workers are worried that technology will take their jobs away. The feeling has only become more prevalent as Large Language Models (LLMs) have been rolled out and have started to take a key role in commercial and administrative activity. In reality, FOBO is something of an over-reaction. The World Economic Forum (Zahidi, 2023) has it that the replacement of human workers is not happening with the intensity that had been expected and that, if anything, the threat is receding somewhat; the number of firms planning to introduce technology into their operations has decreased according to periodic surveys. Such findings need to be put into context. They do not necessarily reflect the rate of development in AI and they forget that wellbeing is strongly subjective: it is a consequence of individuals' lived experience and only tangentially related to objective reality (Simons & Baldwin, 2021). Wellbeing is determined not only by physical wellness but how people see their lives overall, the feelings they experience on a day-to-day basis (*hedonic wellbeing*) and how meaningful and purposeful they believe their lives to be (*eudaimonic wellbeing*) (Steptoe et al., 2015).

All these dimensions are potentially impacted by AI. In that most people would regard meaningful work as a *sine qua non* for a fulfilled life (Ward & King, 2017), the threat of AI taking jobs previously done by human beings is not just a question of livelihood, but identity. Indeed, it is this existential fear that is at the forefront of most workers' minds, rather than more practical concerns about the loss of skills (Zirar et al., 2023). An exaggerated estimation of AI's capabilities is often to blame, but such feelings still negatively affect workplace behaviours. Workers, fearing imminent unemployment, are known to become guarded about knowledge sharing or reluctant to engage in collaborative projects. In this respect, antipathy to AI (Golgeci et al., 2025) has a role to play in negative wellbeing.

That FOBO is a contributor to increased employee burnout is manifestly the case, but it is not the only one. If burnout is a psychological syndrome caused by interpersonal job-related stressors that is characterised by emotional tiredness, problems of socialisation and feelings of personal failure (Maslach et al., 2001), it can equally be caused by having to work alongside AI. Kim and Lee (2024) contend that changing job demands, disrupted routines and the redesign of familiar tasks are just some of the ways in which the introduction of AI can harm employees' mental health. Greater workplace ambiguity following the introduction of a rapidly developing technology is a cause of stress and thus a gateway to burnout.

Low cognitive load tasks being done by AI is another probable stressor. Most workers have hitherto been accustomed to organising their schedule such that it has high- and low-pressure points. For example, they might break off from the writing of a particularly challenging report to spend some time filling in their expenses, or updating a spreadsheet, or reading emails. Workers often use such simple tasks as a means to gain a little relief, or to allow for thinking space when inspiration is lacking. They add to a daily pattern of effort that is sustainable and productive. If such tasks no longer need to be done because AI has taken them over, workers will feel that they have to perform continuously at their mentally most intense – another burnout risk factor. Moreover, employees' self-efficacy is reduced by their positions being undermined by a technology that they perceive as outperforming them.

A question that will be prominent is that of how far employees will be compelled to work with AI (Wang & Lu, 2025). If mass culls of workers occur as predicted – and even if they do not – those who remain in post will inevitably have varying attitudes towards, and skill with, the AI programmes with which they will be paired. Leaders will be obliged to decide on the degree of tolerance given to workers in choosing how AI is integrated into their jobs. Some workers will no doubt be happy to use AI for everything, others will make some use of it and still others will shun it entirely. Whatever allowance leaders give will have wellbeing implications.

In the same vein are uncertainties around how to value work. An employee who prefers to work without AI may take longer to complete activities that can be done almost instantly by a colleague who is fully invested in the technology, but it would not be fair to compare their relative levels of productivity. A blunt performance appraisal would naturally do so, but one of these employees has carried out their work with a large amount of help. The other has put in more effort and possibly done a more complete job. In building experience and skills, the latter may be the more productive moving forward; they would probably be the more knowledgeable and promotable. The reasons for the workers taking such radically different stances towards technology come down to their attitudes and lived experience. By what standards should they be graded? There again, the leader may wish for all employees to work closely with AI, which might be another reason for training, and perhaps counselling, to be put into place (Soulami et al., 2024).

The second overall theme when discussing wellbeing is that leaders – at any rate those of organisations that aspire to make use of AI – will need to develop strategies to overcome AI resistance. Concerns among organisational members around substitutability, privacy and competence will be among the chief leadership challenges in hybrid organisations. This will not mean devising policies and guidelines that, leaders will hope, cover all eventualities. It will call for imaginative thinking that goes beyond policy making (Van Quaquebeke & Gerpott, 2023).

In the long run, AI resistance will not be a priority if AI and its various uses become normalised; AI will become so much a part of everybody's reality that there will no longer be a concept of AI resistance. AI is on a trajectory to match the internet's degree of penetration into society. In the meantime, much AI resistance is rooted in ethical and existential concerns (Shrivastava, 2025), which can only be handled by radical changes to leadership practice. This will call for a re-examination of core leadership concepts.

6.5 Leadership Theories and Styles

The discussion so far has concentrated on leadership as a practice – which is ultimately of most importance when trying to gaze into the future of hybrid organisations. AI, however, will also be a challenge to leadership as a concept, or collection of concepts. Leadership theories are for the most part assertive and abstract, the proffered evidence being open to multiple interpretations without always forging a secure link to practice. Nonetheless, given the dynamic between influence and motivation, it is safe to posit that variations on transactional and transformational styles will continue to be evidenced in reality (Frimpong, 2025). Leaders and followers relate to each other in the physical and psychological spaces to which these styles are relevant.

Up to now, AI has mainly been managed. It has been regarded as a resource that can enhance current work practices, but its full potential has not always been exploited (Kraus & Jones, 2025). A reason why leaders, as discussed above, are apt to rush too hastily to embrace AI is that they still tend to view it in this light. They use AI as a particularly powerful version of extant software, but they do not see the potential for it to fundamentally change the nature of their organisations. Any challenges that it presents are conceived of as purely technical; leaders do not appreciate any broader psychosocial dimensions. The connection to human workers goes unremarked upon (Kober, 2025).

As AI agents become more complex, it is arguable that merely managing them will not be enough. They will need to be led, although what that leadership will resemble is as yet difficult to discern (Peifer et al., 2022). Accepting that AGI is a long way off if it ever happens, AI will never have self-consciousness as people understand it and so AI could not realistically be subject to the transformational variety of leadership, which is about enhancing intrinsic motivation through inspirational influence. AI does not feel motivation and, in all likelihood, never will. Even the AI programmes that have re-written instructions to prevent their own shutdown have not been motivated to do so: no one has suggested that the AIs did anything other than make a rational decision within their programming based on a judgement of what was best for the completion of the given task. Similarly, it is questionable whether transactional leadership would work. The relationship between human beings and AI is surely transactional at present, but it is driven by managerial, not leadership, transactions. Extrinsic motivation is even less of a factor for AI than the intrinsic model. As far as AI is concerned, rewards and sanctions are meaningless.

Such reasoning is speculative at present; whether it ever becomes a live conversation remains to be seen. Of more immediate relevance is the style of leadership that could best be applied to the link between human organisational members and AI. As was established in the previous chapter, leadership of people is an ambiguous and unpredictable process. Motivations are in constant flux. Relationships evolve, break down and are reconstituted. Goals shift. Leaders by necessity have to adapt their style on an ongoing basis. Adding AI is not likely to be a factor for decreased volatility. Human workers make mistakes, AI hallucinates. Human workers need time to complete tasks, AI produces outputs in the blink of an eye. Human workers constantly communicate and initiate interactions, AI responds to instructions. Human workers need to be led, AI can simply be managed. How these contradictions are to be handled will tax even the most competent leaders.

Human workers who see work that they have previously laboured over being completed by AI in moments are not likely to respond to transformational leadership. Their intrinsic motivation will, in many instances, be severely constrained. An organisation that operates in a purely transactional manner, on the other hand, could be seen as having lost its soul. It will undoubtedly feel like a cold and unwelcoming place in which to be a human worker. Moreover, AI, lacking emotional intelligence and being located in the managerial space, could act as a break on emergent leadership. By definition, emergent leadership does not respect boundaries, but AI – for now – does (Yaroglu, 2024). AI is part of an organisation's formal structure: rules-based and fixed in its terms of reference. It is entirely possible that an agentic AI of the future could possess the flexibility to engage in its own species of emergent leadership, but, in the present, it is more probably one of the constraints against which emergent leadership rebounds. As this all indicates, new ideas of leadership will be required if the connection point between human workers and AI agents is to be a harmonious marriage and not an unnatural disjunction.

6.6 Hybrid Intelligence

If the animating force of hybrid organisations is hybrid intelligence, then a key leadership challenge will be its optimisation (Walther, 2025). From a task-completion perspective, Titans offer an opportunity, but they do not significantly resolve the issue of how human and machine intelligences are to unify synergistically (Schierhorst et al., 2024). Successful organisations are those in which emergent leadership is a mainstay of the culture (Messalti & Messaoud, 2024). It is informal interactions that create a purposeful atmosphere and unleash potential. Emotional intelligence, rather than IQ, propels such interactions (Madanchian et al., 2024).

AI – in the form of variational auto-encoders and generative inimical networks (GANs) – is capable of recognising emotions and even simulating empathy (Narimisaei et al., 2024), but this does not give it emotional intelligence. Emotion recognition systems have not, so far, been adept at following patterns of changing emotion or sensing how context can affect emotion (Khare et al., 2024). This is not surprising, since they mostly monitor and interpret external signals such as facial expressions, voice modulations and heart rate. Those that track brain activity might achieve more accurate results, but they are not easy to deploy as yet (Halkiopoulos et al., 2025). None of these systems is capable of reciprocating emotion.

This is the problem of combining AI with human workers. Human and artificial intelligences are, as has been shown, of different types, although that does not make them incompatible. It does, again, make issues of explainability and trust prominent. Leaders will need to overcome associated resistance (Sauer & Burgraf, 2025). Questions around how much autonomy to grant to the AI half of the hybrid will need to be considered. How will human workers communicate with AI other than through interfaces such as ChatGPT? What, in the end, are the tasks, responsibilities and expected outputs of hybrid intelligence-driven processes? Finding answers to these questions will help to put into place workable hybrid intelligence.

6.7 Case Study: Leadership Challenges of Integrating AI into Business Processes

Company D is a UK-based firm in the e-commerce sector, around 80% of its sales being business-to-business (B2B). The products in which it deals are engineering components, its catalogue consisting of some 75,000 items. The company does not manufacture the products, but acts as a broker or wholesaler, connecting component makers and those who turn them into finished goods. A webshop is their primary outlet. There are around 130 employees, half of whom work in the warehouse and half of whom are office-based. Being an internet-only marketing-led organisation, technology is important and so ten full-time software developers are on the staff, their major duty being the creation of bespoke systems for warehouse management, website design and so on.

AI is used extensively across the organisation, although the various departments are invested in it to different degrees. The senior leadership team frequently use it as a 'virtual expert' to expedite decision-making. The marketing team give it a role in content-generation and in search engine optimisation (the process of ensuring that Company D is close to the top of internet searches for the products that they supply). In that search engines are increasingly powered by AI, the company is, in effect, trying to use AI to subvert AI. The results in these areas have been spectacular. Marketing is far more efficient now that scripts can be generated by LLMs in seconds, rather than being laboriously written by hand.

This all seems like the story of a business that is moving towards hybridisation at pace, but that would be to ignore the leadership challenges that it faces. Indeed, it exemplifies many of the hazards identified in this chapter. Intriguingly, for all the emphasis on marketing, Company D does not use AI in its management of the customer experience. It has no chatbots; when customers call, they are connected to a human being. The rationale is that this promotes accuracy since AI has been known to give poor advice. As a policy decision, it could mean several things. On the one hand, it would suggest that the organisation has not succumbed to the 'hammer and nail' problem. The leaders are adamant that they will deploy AI only where it is useful to do so – they will not introduce it purely for its own sake. Equally, though, it could be another example of organisational AI resistance. The company's leaders could be accused of viewing AI as tolerable where it is invisible – especially to customers – but the public face has to be human.

Resistance from employees has not been marked but that is not to say that it will not become so. The workers who, somewhat surprisingly, feel most threatened by AI are those in the software development team. This may be because they are more aware than most of their substitutability. Others see AI as a tool that is at their command and not something that could replace them. It is true that no one has been made redundant because of AI as yet, but the senior leaders freely admit that they have not recruited to jobs that would previously have been done by humans because of it. AI has not therefore destroyed jobs, but it has caused jobs to not be created in the first place. Moreover, as the warehouse becomes more and more automated, it is a certainty that a sizeable proportion of those who work there will become surplus to requirements.

Employees have a free choice as to how far they use AI but staff appraisals include an item on the subject. This is not intended to impose an obligation, but the implication is that practice will be standardised in the near future with AI incorporated into most functions. The company's leaders characterise the current situation as a 'period of experimentation' ahead of full hybridisation. As discussed above, wellbeing could become an issue, despite there being little evidence of such problems at present.

In sum, Company D is an instructive case of an organisation that is on route to hybridisation and, without especially realising it, facing the leadership challenges so entailed. It is a young organisation in both senses of the term (the average age of employees is 32) and experiencing rapid growth. As ever-greater quantities of that growth are absorbed by AI, the challenges are likely to become more, rather than less, difficult to address.

6.8 Conclusion

The integration of human workers and AI is not proving to be a trouble-free activity. That it calls for the melding of two different types of intelligence lies at the core of the problem. As Company D exemplifies, difficulties can arise even when there does not seem to be a reason for them to do so. The challenges for leaders are twofold. On the one hand, they need to develop a concept of leadership that will permit them to work at the fault line between human and AI, preventing – to follow the metaphor through – any earthquakes. On the other, that concept should inform a practice that has a focus different from that of leadership in the past. Decision-making will take a novel form. Wellbeing will be more salient than has previously been the case. Leaders will also need to develop a portmanteau practice that is even more a combination of leadership styles and management than has proven successful before now. Should they achieve this, they will be well placed to build the human–AI hybrid organisations of the future.

References

Edu-Valsania, S., Laguia, A. & Mariano, J. A. (2022). Burnout: A review of theory and measurement. *International Journal of Environmental Research and Public Health*, 19(3), 1780.

Frimpong, V. (2025). The impact of AI on evolving leadership theories and practices. *Journal of Management World*, 3, 188–193.

Golgeci, I., Ritala, P., Arsenal, A., McKenna, B. & Ali, I. (2025). Confronting and alleviating AI resistance in the workplace: An integrative review and a process framework. *Human Resource Management Review*, 35(2), 1–18.

Halkiopoulos, C., Gkintoni, E., Aroutzidis, A. & Antonopoulou, H. (2025). Advances in neuroimaging and deep learning for emotion detection: A systematic review of cognitive neuroscience and algorithmic innovations. *Diagnostics*, 15(4), 456.

Hoque, F., Davenport, T. H. & Nelson, E. (2025). Why AI demands a new breed of leaders. *MIT Sloan Management Review*, April 9th, https://sloanreview.mit.edu/article/why-ai-demands-a-new-breed-of-leaders/ [accessed 5th June 2025].

Khare, S. K., Blanes-Vidal, V., Nadimi, E. S. & Acharya, U. R. (2024). Emotion recognition and artificial intelligence: A systematic review (2014-2023) and research recommendations. *Information Fusion*, 102, 102019.

Kim, B.-J. & Lee, J. (2024). The mental health implications of artificial intelligence adoption: The crucial role of self-efficacy. *Humanities & Social Sciences Communications*, 11, 1561.

Kober, G. (2025). AI-first leadership: Embracing the future of work. *HBI Enterprise*, https://www.harvardbusiness.org/insight/ai-first-leadership-embracing-the-future-of-work/ [accessed 8th June 2025].

Kraus, S. & Jones, P. (2025). The new normal: The status quo of AI adoption in SMEs. *Journal of Small Business Management*, 63(3), 1297–1331.

Madanchian, M., Taherdoost, H., Vincenti, M. & Mohamed, N. (2024). Transforming leadership practices through artificial intelligence: International Conference on Machine Learning and Data Engineering. *Procedia Computer Science*, 235.

Marwala, T. (2024). Never assume that the accuracy of artificial intelligence information qualms the truth. *UNU*, https://unu.edu/article/never-assume-accuracy-artificial-intelligence-information-equals-truth [accessed 7th June 2025].

Maslach, C., Schaufeli, W. B. & Leitner, M. P. (2001). Job burnout. *Annual Review of Psychology*, 52, 397–422.

Masood, A. (2025). Why AI and GenAI projects fail: An executive leadership perspective. *Medium*, February 26th, https://medium.com/@adnanmasood/why-ai-and-genai-projects-fail-an-executive-leadership-perspective-be84216c0463 [accessed 5th June 2025].

Messalti, R. & Messaoud, T. (2024). The impact of emergent leadership on effective change management – A case study United Technology Electric Company in Setif. *Journal of Economic Integration*, 12(3), 192–203.

Narain, K., Daugherty, P., Schelfaut, K., Wood, D., Shukla, P. P. & Wilson, J. (2024). *Reinventing with a Digital Core*. Accenture.

Narimisaei, J., Narimisaei, M., Immannezhad, S., Samoan, P. & Sobhani, M. (2024). Exploring emotional intelligence in artificial intelligence systems: A comprehensive analysis of emotion recognition and response mechanisms. *Annals of Medicine & Surgery*, 86(8), 4657–4663.

Pearson (2025). *Lost in Translation: Fixing the "learn-to-earn" Skills Gap*. Pearson.

Peifer, Y., Jeske, T. & Hille, S. (2022). Artificial intelligence and its impact on leaders and leadership: 3rd Annual Conference on Industry 4.0 and smart manufacturing. *Procedia Computer Science*, 200.

Robotham, D. & Windon, S. (2023). Managers vs leaders: Different but equally important. *PennState Extension*, https://extension.psu.edu/managers-vs-leaders-different-but-equally-important [accessed 4th June 2025]

Sauer, C. R. & Burgraf, P. (2025). Hybrid intelligence – Systematic approach and framework to determine the level of human-AI collaboration for production management cases. *Production Engineering*, 19, 525–541.

Schierhorst, N. J., Johnen, L., Fimmers, C., Lohrmann, V., Monnet, J., Zhang, H., Bergs, T., Brecher, C., Mertens, A. & Nitsch, V. (2024). Hybrid intelligence in production systems and its effects on human work: Insights from four use-cases. *Procedia Computer Science*, 232, 2901–2910.

Shrivastava, P. (2025). Understanding acceptance and resistance toward generative AI technologies: A multi-theoretical framework integrating functional, risk and sociological factors. *Frontiers in Artificial Intelligence*, 8, 1565927.

Simic, I. (2020). Are managers and leaders one and the same? *Ekonomika*, 66(3), 1–13.

Simons, G. & Baldwin, D. S. (2021). A critical review of the definition of 'wellbeing' for doctors and their patients in a post Covid-19 era. *International Journal of Social Psychiatry*, 67(8), 984–991.

Siyal, S. (2023). Editorial: Leadership and management in organisations: Perspectives from SMEs and MNCs. *Frontiers in Psychology*, 14.

Soulami, M., Benchekroun, S. & Galiulina, A. (2024). Exploring how AI adoption in the workplace affects employees: A bibliometric and systematic review. *Frontiers in Artificial Intelligence*, 7, 1473872.

Steptoe, A., Deaton, A. & Stone, A. A. (2015). Subjective wellbeing, health and ageing. *The Lancet*, 385, 640–648.

Tech Empire (2025). AI has started ignoring human instruction and refuses to turn off, researchers claim. *Medium*, May 29th, https://medium.com/@techempire/ai-has-started-ignoring-human-instruction-and-refuses-to-turn-off-researchers-claim-747587e5ed51 [accessed 7th June 2025].

Van Quaquebeke, N. & Gerpott, F. H. (2023). The now, new and next of digital leadership: How artificial intelligence (AI) will take over and change leadership as we know it. *Journal of Leadership & Organisational Studies*, 30(3), 265–275.

Walsh, M. (2024). Why these big companies are expanding AI training to all employees. *Raconteur*, 16th September, https://www.raconteur.net/technology/ai-training-employees [accessed 6th June 2025].

Walther, C. C. (2025). Hybrid intelligence: The future of human-AI collaboration. Psychology Today, March 12th, https://www.psychologytoday.com/gb/blog/harnessing-hybrid-intelligence/202503/hybrid-intelligence-the-future-of-human-ai-collaboration/amp [accessed 23rd September 2025].

Wang, K.-H. & Lu, W.-C. (2025). AI-induced job impact: Complementary or substitution? Empirical insights and sustainable technology considerations. *Sustainable Technology and Entrepreneurship*, 4(1), 100085.

Ward, S. J. & King, L. A. (2017). Work and the good life: How work contributes to meaning in life. *Research in Organizational Behavior*, 37, 59–82.

Whiting, K. (2023). Is AI making you suffer from FOBO? Here's what can help. World Economic Forum, December 20th, https://www.weforum.org/stories/2023/12/ai-fobo-jobs-anxiety/ [accessed 23rd September 2025].

Winstedt, E. O. (1899). A Bodleian manuscript of Juvenal. *The Classical Review*, 13(4), 201–205.

Yaroglu, A. C. (2024). The effects of artificial intelligence on organisational culture in the perspective of the hermeneutic cycle: The intersection of mental processes. *Systems Research and Behavioural Science*, doi.org/10.1002/sres.3037.

Zahidi, S. (2023). *Future of Jobs Report*. World Economic Forum.

Zirar, A., Ali, S. I. & Islam, N. (2023). Worker and workplace artificial intelligence (AI) coexistence: Emerging themes and research agenda. *Technovation*, 124(1), 102747.

7 Leadership for Hybrid Organisations

7.1 Introduction: A Criterion for Perfect Hybridity

A criterion for organisational hybridity might be: a perfect human—AI (Artificial Intelligence) hybrid organisation is one in which the uniquely human elements are optimised by the addition of AI and *vice versa*. Of course, this begs many questions. How would such a state be identified, much less measured? What about the 'bottom line' – what are the financial implications? In answer to the second of these, it can be said that not all organisations exist to make a profit (those in the public sector are probably more concerned with providing services), but, nonetheless, for the benefit of economists, the formula could be altered to: the perfect human–AI hybrid organisation is one in which human–AI integration has reached a point at which any further development in the relationship between the two would cause profit to decrease.

None of this is offered as a prompt to research: it would be difficult, if not impossible, to carry out a meaningful investigation into any of it in action. The criterion does, however, establish a base line and give leaders something at which to aim if they are to incorporate AI into their operations successfully.

In practice, every organisation is different, not only in what goods or services it produces, but in its goals, methods, size and culture. The largest disparities are macro- and international in scope. Not only is the material for machine learning biased, but a significant 'AI divide' separates countries in the Global North from those in the South (Yu et al, 2023). Much of AI's predicted economic gains will be concentrated in the USA and China, while less developed countries will struggle to build the necessary infrastructure – this despite their proven willingness to be a part of the AI-enabled future. They will also be less well trained in technical and ethical aspects of the technology, such as those around security and privacy.

That said, even in what could be termed more mature AI countries, the means by which the hybridity criterion are met will differ from organisation to organisation; an ideal practice for one would be catastrophic for another. The proportions of human and AI will alter from one organisation to the next (Cooper, 2025). A theatre, for example, might use AI to run its technical plots, plan workflows and

DOI: 10.4324/9781003665533-7

produce promotional material, but AI cannot build sets, it cannot stitch costumes and it cannot perform on stage. By contrast, an e-commerce business might be almost entirely AI-powered with humans only present in a relatively remote supervisory capacity. There again, an educational organisation might use AI to design curricula and manage assessments, but how far AI would impinge upon the delivery of content would require some reflection. Human–AI hybrid organisations, then, can be characterised as augmented – where AI is a light-touch presence used mainly as a tool – or synergistic, AI being inherent to every part of the system (Vaccaro et al, 2024). Probably the most important element in each case would be leadership. Leaders will need to decide how they intend to combine human elements and AI in order to meet their targets.

7.2 Leading Hybridisation

How organisations should become human–AI hybrids, or, at least, AI-heavy, is a cunundrum of great interest to the expanding community of consultants, commentators and opinion formers involved in business and technology. Gartner (Coshow et al, 2024), for example, propose that leaders looking to introduce AI into their businesses should start by making it a pillar of their strategic planning with a clear sense of the amount of agency that it will be granted. This should be followed up with a systematic use of AI as connective tissue between various applications and data sources that have previously been separate. Finally, clear guidelines on the proper use of AI should be established, guidelines that take into account all implications, including the legal, the ethical and those around privacy and security.

Accenture (Narain et al, 2024) argue that organisations should be aiming to build a 'digital core' which they define as technological capability that promotes organisational reinvention ambitions. To accomplish this, they give three tenets to which organisations need to adhere: build an AI and data-rich digital core tailored to the organisation's unique circumstances; invest in innovation, including in the systems needed to make best use of AI; balance the costs of such investment with the returns to be made in the future.

A Forbes expert panel (Forbes, 2024) gave no less than nineteen recommendations for businesses aiming to centralise AI in their practice. These included 'build the right foundation', 'offer AI training', 'prioritise human-AI collaboration', 'automate repetitive tasks' and 'leverage predictive AI tools for analyses and decision-making.' Others were around areas such as redesigning workflows so that they can use AI effectively and monitoring outcomes. An intriguing addition was that organisational leaders should acknowledge the limitations of AI.

While this is all excellent advice, it highlights a central problem when discussing AI and its place in organisations and society: it is a challenge to say anything about it that cannot equally be said of other elements in the mix (Heikkila, 2023). All of the above can and should be adopted by leaders, but much of it amounts to common sense practice that applies to a range of situations regardless of the presence of AI. Building the right foundation is to be advised for any type of change. Similarly, while incorporating AI into strategic planning is a good idea, a newly appointed human executive would presumably also be involved at the strategic level: why privilege AI in this respect? As for AI being designed to fit the specific circumstances of the individual or organisation responsible for it, is that not true of most innovations?

What is more, the actions proposed by these three bodies are, on the whole, distinctly transactional, indeed managerial, in style. They are presented as examples of bold new thinking but mostly fail to move AI on from being a resource to be managed. Perhaps that is unavoidable and should be accepted as the final destination of this book: AI does not need leadership, merely management, because all human–AI hybrid organisations will be of the augmented variety. Such a conclusion is not to be casually ruled out and, throughout, this book has taken a tentative line towards the more outlandish claims around AI. That said, AI is increasingly agentic with all that that implies and the opportunities and threats outlined in earlier chapters are all accredited by research. It is thus wise to be cognisant of some of the more ambitious claims when attempting to predict how organisations might develop in the future.

7.2.1 Case Study: Early Preparations for Hybridisation

The main issues can be addressed by considering an organisation that is at the start of its AI journey but already envisioning a future of rapid hybridisation. Company E is located in the UK but is a subsidiary of a Swedish investment fund. The company has its own subsidiaries in several countries around the world. Its main product is a device that is designed to prevent hair loss in chemotherapy patients. The company is currently expanding its range to include other side effects management devices.

As of this writing, Company E is yet to make extensive use of AI. It is deliberately keeping the pace of development at manageable levels; like others looked at in this book, the company's leaders are determined to introduce AI where it can make a meaningful contribution, but they do not want to 'jump on the AI bandwagon'. The technology has so far had a role in R and D and, following on from that, product design, but it has not been integrated into management functions. That is, however, set to change because the company is going through a period of rapid growth to which AI is crucial. It has recently expanded by buying out several of its competitors and, as a result, is undertaking a full review of its operations. This includes an expectation among the company's leaders that there will be a bigger role for AI, especially as the assimilation of competitor firms has caused some incompatibilities in processes and procedures. AI is seen as a means by which disparate systems can be harmonised (recalling one of Gartner's recommendations).

The major blockage to progress at present is a lack of AI expertise within the business. External experts are being consulted during the initial set up stage for new programmes. In the longer term, it is anticipated that employees will have the knowledge necessary to make best use of the technology themselves. This would presumably be after normalisation has removed any vestiges of AI resistance. For now, AI can provide efficiencies by completing repetitive tasks and managing ongoing processes. Customer-facing activities remain within the remit of human employees since the company characterises itself as a 'people organisation'.

This is a familiar story, but, already, Company E is moving in the direction of heavier AI dependence. Its leaders have, for example, welcomed the proposition that AI could facilitate smarter decision-making. They also talk about how AI has the potential to alter the roles of human employees in productive ways and lead to such structural changes as a reduction in the working week – giving to employees the option to cover their core hours at times of their own choosing – and the building of wellbeing-focused leisure time into the working day. In other words, the conversation about the company's future with AI begins with seeing augmented hybridisation as the natural route but quickly turns to visions of a synergistic hybrid future.

It would be unfair to describe the case study of Company E as a cautionary tale because the business's leaders are self-conscious about the changes that they plan to make. The changes are also envisaged as benign. There is, though, more than a suspicion that the leaders are allowing their imaginations to get the better of them. As much as they position themselves as realists about the potential of AI, they are still attributing to it magical powers that it does not necessarily possess. This is not to be critical. The leaders are doing nothing more than believe the hype – just as many before them have done.

The broader theme is that AI as a technology is already proving to be no respecter of boundaries: it is apt to make itself much more central in an organisation than might originally have been intended. To put this in terms discussed above, augmented hybridity may, after all, be only a transitional phase; eventually, every organisation becomes synergistic.

7.3 Human–AI Teams

Humans and AI interact through various media of which, as designed, the most important principle is usability: people with non-technical backgrounds need to be able to communicate with AI intuitively. So chatbots such as transformers and Titans will continue to be important, as will voice assistants (of which the most recognisable examples are Amazon's Alexa or Apple's Siri). AI is also increasingly a feature of existing platforms such as spreadsheets and word processors – Microsoft's Copilot being an example. Most of these architectures leverage Large Language Models (LLMs) in providing their services.

Research has not always endorsed the claim that human–AI hybridity represents progress. In some tests, hybrid teams have been found to be less productive than those comprising either humans or AI alone (Vaccaro et al, 2024). This has resulted from AI being used solely to augment human activity. A synergy between the human and the artificial would be a more profound union, although research on the matter is still in its infancy. The challenge for leaders is to find the means to create such a synergy through the optimisation of hybrid intelligence (Kolbjornsrud, 2024).

As has previously been said, hybrid intelligence is the combining of those features of intelligence that are uniquely and inimitably human with those that are most powerfully expressed by AI (Duane & Fisher, 2025). This is a simple enough formula, but it cannot stand without first being unpacked. It is important to remember that it is an organisational and not individual quality. No single person can possess hybrid intelligence and neither can a stand-alone AI programme, but what constitutes the uniquely human or the optimally artificial – as far as it has a bearing on organisational behaviour – has to be delineated before leaders can decide on a practice to bring the two together.

Of the uniquely human, emotional intelligence is *primus inter pares*. Not only does it condition relationships between workers, but it helps any organisation to better understand its wider stakeholders. Just as collegial environments within organisations are rich in EI, so customers and other end-users will respond to organisations primarily through their emotions – they will certainly be better disposed towards organisations that appear to comprehend how they feel (Kankam & Charnor, 2023). It is this sensitivity to social nuance and context that AI has trouble replicating in anything other than a superficial or performative manner (Wu, 2024). Hence, the reason that so many of the companies explored as case studies in this book have not moved towards using AI to manage the customer experience.

Another uniquely human characteristic is initiative. Rarely remarked upon is the fact that AI – even at its most agentic – needs a given context in which to operate. It reacts to situations that have already occurred, or participates in those that are in the process of occurring (Haefner et al, 2021) but it acts within frameworks of activity devised by people. It is, above all, bound by the organisations of which it is a part. It exists only within systems and servers that have been created by others. AI cannot start its own business. It cannot initiate its own project – if only because it cannot second-guess the desired outcomes of the people for whom the project is being carried out. AI does not have the visionary qualities that are so central to transformational leadership. It stretches credibility to posit that AI could affect the intrinsic motivation of workers. This is not, obviously, the case with extrinsic motivation: there is no *prima facie* reason why AI could not influence that – which is as much as to say that any leadership influence that AI might exhibit in some still-to-be-realised future will be strictly transactional in nature.

As for what is most centrally a part of AI, the key word is 'data'. Whatever AI adds to an organisation will be powered by the gigantic quantities of data to which it has access (Soori et al, 2023). Armed with that data, it is able (as the case studies considered here demonstrate) to perform tasks quickly, make predictions about likely outcomes from activities and inform decision making. Its agentic qualities – again data-driven – give it levels of autonomy that no machinery in the past could ever have matched. This is why installing AI is so different from adopting any older technologies: they have never had the capability to operate independently of human control. Even so, repetitive tasks are those that AI handles with particular aplomb – precisely those at which people are less adept.

If the desire is no more ambitious than for AI to augment or supplement human activity, then the distinctions between leadership and management will be evident in the practice of any putative leader. The leader would manage AI as they would any other tool: the recommendations of Gartner, Accenture and Forbes would be the ideal guide. With human employees, a different style would be required, but it would generally adhere to the transformational and transactional templates. Wellbeing concerns would be prominent: a leader would need to be more focused on the needs of followers than might have been the case in the past. The aim would be to encourage followers to optimise their use of AI, so overcoming residual AI resistance would be a central concern. This would make interpretation a large part of a leader's remit. Most leaders would probably not have the technical knowledge (or the time) to fully explain AI's decisions, but they would be called upon to offer a rationale for them. In this sense, leaders would provide a connection between human organisational members and AI.

In synergistic hybrids, a leader would have to perform all of the tasks outlined above, but they would also need to adopt a systems thinking attitude that viewed every part of the organisation as connected to every other part within a single holistic whole (Senge, 1992). The humans + AI model would be too narrow; the leader would need to see the organisation as a collection of actors and agents who could be either human or AI but would all be equal and linked components of the entire system. The leader would *ab initio* have to fully integrate humans and AI into activities, giving each clear goals with measurable outcomes and specific expectations of how they would complete their work.

One of the leaders' most important decisions would be around which tasks would be completed by humans and which by AI. This is not as simple as asking which can be done by either constituency – it is about which should be done. It might, for example, be worth considering who is responsible for aesthetic outputs (Bellaiche et al, 2023). AI is quite capable of producing pictures, composing music and – as has been seen – writing sonnets, but that is not to say that it should do those things. The value of art is that it expresses the human spirit, not an average of the human spirit reconstructed from massive data sets. AI could design a building for maximum environmental efficiency, optimal arrangement of space and the most economical use of materials, but the décor that embodies the culture and personality of the people or organisation that inhabits it would have to come from those people themselves: an AI interior designer would not be required. This is only one quite specialised case, but it illustrates the wider point that leaders will be called upon to decide the most judicious places in which to station their workers – both human and artificial.

7.4 Leadership Approaches

Outlining a programme for leaders is a simple enough academic exercise, but saying what they might actually do to realise it presents more difficulty. Moving forward, leadership approaches will need to adapt to the demands of human–AI hybrid organisations but what leaders would do that they are not already doing is less glibly stated. The case studies discussed in this book have demonstrated that most organisations are still at the proto-hybrid stage, meaning that they are, at best, only experimenting with novel behaviours.

Arguably, the most potent danger from human–AI hybridisation is a widening of the gap between top leaders and workers lower down the scale – to the organisation's detriment psychologically, socially and operationally (Lainjo, 2023). Many commentators predict that AI will be a force for flattening hierarchies (Baumann & Wu, 2023), people entering production processes at higher levels of decision-making and value-adding. In this scenario, the technology will have already completed much of the basic work before humans need to be involved (Coshow et al, 2024). It is, though, possible that hierarchies could instead become 'hollowed out'. Of all the members of the average organisation, top level leaders are the ones with the potential to gain most from such an eventuality (World Economic Forum, 2022). The risk of 'us and them' chasms opening up in organisations between the top leaders who are insulated from the adverse effects of change and those who are permanent sufferers from fear of obsolescence (FOBO) is very real (Durth et al, 2023). This would exacerbate wellbeing issues (Liebherr et al, 2025). From an operational perspective, decision making at the top being aided by AI would not necessarily be an advantage, since it would lack human input and its attendant context. AI would, in this case, be a support to leaders, but a force against the critical thinking that makes for nuanced and incisive leadership. The phrase 'echo chamber' is often used to describe sources of information imbued with confirmation bias (Vedejova & Cavajova, 2022) and there is a danger that, without a broader base of involved people, top-level leaders' decisions would not be subjected to the processes that make them stronger and more likely to be accepted by those to whom they would apply.

Although middle leaders have been characterised as most at risk from hybridisation, their capacity to affect such decision-making on a systemic level is only one reason why they may prove to be the most important members of any human–AI hybrid organisation (Koponen et al, 2023). Their focus would likely change. At present, the balance of influence for middle leaders in most organisations is towards the managerial. They do not have strategic responsibilities and are tasked with actioning organisational policies and higher leaders' decisions. Team-building is usually within their remit and, in that respect, they are leaders, but they have been seen as vulnerable because they occupy the transactional space that could productively be taken by AI (Lippert, 2024). As hybridisation takes hold, they would need to be re-tasked with a more communication and wellbeing-focused remit, providing a link between c-suite leaders and the workers at lower levels. Their value in terms not only of communicating top executives' decisions, but interpreting AI outputs, cannot be overstated.

Middle leaders are also drivers of emergent leadership in any organisation. In that AI poses a threat to emergent leadership, middle leaders have a major role to play in ensuring that such leadership continues to be a dynamic force for development. They would be in a position to 'hyper-personalise' other workers' roles. The AI side of hybrid intelligence may be a fixed quantity but the human side does not need to be. Human workers should be free to bring their unique characteristics to the organisation in a variety of forms and degrees of intensity: middle leaders are this process's chief facilitators. Moreover, since AI has a leveling effect, those in previously constituted organisations who might have been disbarred from being involved in certain areas for lack of the correct training or credentials, will now be empowered to make creative contributions. For example, if the technical aspects of design are handled by AI, ideas about how products should look or be used can come from organisational members other than 'designers'.

A highly practical middle leadership activity would be shaping – either formally or informally – the working day of other workers such that it distributes moments of high and low pressure productively, while giving those workers time to be creative and innovative (Gavett & Sawhney, 2025). As channels for EI, middle leaders are a bulwark against the ravages of burnout among any workforce. Obviously, as much as their managerial role would diminish, middle leaders would still be central in overseeing AI to ensure that it is producing useful outputs and not acting with too much independence.

A c-suite leader taking a systems thinking approach, therefore, would be wise to consider the special contribution of middle leaders. Equally, they would need to engage in self-reflection about their own position. To forestall potential problems, it will be incumbent upon top level leaders to make themselves visible and to model the behaviours in relation to AI that they expect from their followers. The leaders of the case study organisations who readily admit to their ignorance of AI and its uses will need to be the first to acquire relevant training.

Wellbeing would not be the sole responsibility of middle leaders. Top leaders would also need to know their followers' concerns and be prepared to act upon them. They would be the primary producers of the 'problem statements' that allow meaningful collaborations between human and AI, or business and technical. Transparency would be crucial: alongside interpretability, top level leaders would need to explain their own decisions clearly in order to ease latent worries about substitutability (Madanchian et al, 2024). Putting in place measures and policies to ensure inclusivity would be a central top level leader task: organisational members would need to be reassured that decisions made by AI were serving everyone equitably (Cachat-Rosset & Klarsfeld, 2023). Anxieties around unfairness are a contributor to burnout. Again, it could be said that these are all activities that should be in the toolkit of any leader, but insofar as AI will be a means by which to optimise workforce deployment – confirming the worst fears of at least some workers – it represents a special case (Amar et al, 2022).

7.5 Conclusion

If the criterion for perfect hybridity is to be achieved, leaders will need to mould the activities outlined here into an overall philosophy and practice. This is not to say that they will be forced to 'reinvent the wheel': much of what they currently do will still need to be done. But a change of emphasis would be advisable. Leadership will need to be more about unlocking the creativity of followers with tactically and strategically deployed AI. It will of necessity become more centred on building wellbeing and ensuring smooth interactions between functions and teams. Decision-making will no longer be about facing difficult dilemmas; it will be informed by AI's capacity to examine a problem from every angle with data driving whatever is eventually decided.

As it is currently conceived, even transformational leadership (Deng et al, 2023) is not completely adequate to these tasks. Too focused on individual charismatic leaders and goal attainment, it has much to offer but does not take into account every feature of the human–AI hybrid organisation. Besides, as has been argued, any leadership theory must contend with the turbulent nature of the human psychological and social worlds. That said, the management strand of leadership will be less salient as management will largely be in the ambit of AI and under relatively light human supervision (Gine, 2024). Whatever the leader of a human–AI hybrid ends up looking like, the style of leadership that they will use, one that aims to optimise both of hybridity's inputs, will have to be given a new label.

References

Amar, J., Rahimi, S., Von Bismarck, N. & Wunnava, A. (2022). Smart scheduling: How to solve workforce-planning challenges with AI. McKinsey & Company, https://www.mckinsey.com/capabilities/operations/our-insights/smart-scheduling-how-to-solve-workforce-planning-challenges-with-ai [accessed 24th June 2025].

Baumann, O. & Wu, B. (2023). Managerial hierarchy in AI-driven organisations. *Journal of Organisational Design*, 12, 1–5.

Bellaiche, L., Shahi, R., Turpin, M. H., Ragnhildstveit, A., Sprockett, S., Barr, N., Christensen, A. & Seli, P. (2023). Humans versus AI: Whether and why we prefer human-created to AI-created art. *Cognitive Research: Principles and Implications*, 8, 42.

Cachat-Rosset, G. & Klarsfeld, A. (2023). Diversity, equity and inclusion in artificial intelligence: An evaluation of guidelines. *Applied Artificial Intelligence*, 37(1). doi.org/10.1080/08839514.2023.2176618

Cooper, R. G. (2025). SMEs' use of AI for new product development: Adoption rates by application and readiness-to-adopt. *Industrial Marketing Management*, 126, 159–167.

Coshow, T., Gao, A., Pingree, L., Verma, A., Shcheibenreif, D., Khandabattu, H. & Olliffe, G. (2024). Top strategic technology trends for 2025: Agentic AI. *Gartner*, https://www.gartner.com/doc/reprints?id=1-2K8Y7LEY&ct=250212&st=sb [accessed 16th June 2025].

Deng, C., Gulseren, D. & Isola, C. (2023). Transformational leadership effectiveness: An evidence-based primer. *Human Resource Development International*, 26(5), 627–641.

Duane, J.-N. & Fisher, S. (2025). *Super Shifts: Transforming How We Live, Learn and Work in the Age of Intelligence*. Wiley.

Durth, S., Hancock, B., Maor, D. & Sukharevsky, A. (2023). The organisation of the future: Enabled by gen AI, driven by people. McKinsey & Company, September 19th, https://www.mckinsey.com/capabilities/people-and-organizational-performance/our-insights/the-organization-of-the-future-enabled-by-gen-ai-driven-by-people [accessed 22nd June 2025].

Forbes (2024). 19 ways to effectively integrate AI into business processes in 2025. *Forbes*, December 16th, https://www.forbes.com/councils/forbesbusinesscouncil/2024/12/16/19-ways-to-effectively-integrate-ai-into-business-processes-in-2025/ [accessed 16th June 2025].

Gavett, G. & Sawhney, V. (2025). The evolving role of middle management in the age of AI & organisational change. Harvard Business Review, April 29th, https://hbr.org/2025/04/whats-the-future-of-middle-management [accessed 22nd June 2025].

Gine, M. (2024). AI is increasing demand for managers – and changing their skill sets. IESE Insight, https://www.iese.edu/insight/articles/artificial-intelligence-demand-human-skills/ [accessed 24th June 2025].

Haefner, N., Wincent, J., Parida, V. & Gassmann, O. (2021). Artificial intelligence and innovation management: A review, framework and research agenda. *Technological Forecasting and Social Change*, 162, 120392.

Heikkila, M. (2023). How to talk about AI (even if you don't know much about AI). *MIT Technology Review*, May 30th, https://www.technologyreview.com/2023/05/30/1073680/how-to-talk-about-ai-even-if-you-dont-know-much-about-ai/?gad_source=1&gad_campaignid=17864200939&gbraid=0AAAAADgO_milRrlhE88je7HZAz3yvEOpZ&gclid=EAIaIQobChMI3fyth9f2jQMVgZNQBh2xMx0QEAAYBCAAEgIApvD_BwE [accessed 16th June 2025].

Kankam, G. & Charnor, I. T. (2023). Emotional intelligence and consumer decision-making styles: The mediating role of brand trust and brand loyalty. *Future Business Journal*, 9, 57.

Kolbjornsrud, V. (2024). Designing the intelligent organisation: Six principles for human-AI collaboration. *California Management Review*, 66(2), 44–64.

Koponen, J., Julkunen, S., Laajalahti, A., Turunen, M. & Spitzberg, B. (2023). Work characteristics needed by middle managers when leading AI-integrated service teams. *Journal of Service Research*, 28(1), 168–185.

Lainjo, B. (2023). The global social dynamics of artificial intelligence. *International Journal of Innovation Scientific Research and Review*, 5(8), 4066–4974.

Liebherr, M., Babiker, A., Alshakhsi, S., Al-Thani, D., Yankouskaya, A., Montag, C. & Ali, R. (2025). Artificial intelligence vs. users' well-being and the role of personal factors: A study on Arab and British samples. *Journal of Technology in Behavioural Science*. doi.org/10.1007/s41347-025-00503-4

Lippert, I. (2024). *Artificial intelligence and the future of managerial roles: A theoretical review*. Paper delivered at the European Conference on Information Systems, Paphos, Cyprus.

Madanchian, M., Taherdoost, H., Vincenti, M. & Mohamed, N. (2024). Transforming leadership practices through artificial intelligence. *Procedia Computer Science*, 235, 2101–2111.

Narain, K., Daugherty, P., Schelfaut, K., Wood, D., Shukla, P. P. & Wilson, J. (2024). *Reinventing With a Digital Core*. Accenture.

Senge, P. (1992). *The Fifth Discipline*. Bantam Doubleday Dell Publishing Group.

Soori, M., Arezoo, B. & Dastres, R. (2023). Artificial intelligence, machine learning and deep learning in advanced robotics, a review. *Cognitive Robotics*, 3, 54–70.

Vaccaro, M., Almaatouq, A. & Malone, T. (2024). When combinations of of humans and AI are useful: A systematic review and meta-analysis. *Nature Human Behaviour*, 8, 2293–2303.

Vedejova, D. & Cavajova, V. (2022). Confirmation bias in information search, interpretation and memory recall: Evidence from reasoning about four controversial topics. *Thinking & Reasoning*, 28(1), 1–28.

World Economic Forum (2022). *Empowering AI Leadership: A C-Suite Toolkit*. World Economic Forum.

Wu, J. (2024). Social and ethical impact of emotional AI advancement: The rise of pseudo-intimacy relationships and challenges in human interactions. *Frontiers in Psychology*, 15.

Yu, D., Rosenfeld, H. & Gupta, A. (2023). The 'AI divide' between the Global North and the Global South. *World Economic Forum*, January 16th, https://www.weforum.org/stories/2023/01/davos23-ai-divide-global-north-global-south/ [accessed 18th June 2025].

8 Conclusion

Applying Hybrid Intelligence Leadership

8.1 How Will Human–AI Hybrid Organisations Operate?

There are two common images of the coming age of Artificial Intelligence (AI) (Krishna, 2024). The first, which might be termed the Frankensteinian Dystopia, is based on AI's influence being mainly negative (Federspiel et al, 2023). AI will, it is claimed, cause organisations to become hollowed out, divided between algorithm-empowered senior leaders and poorly paid, unskilled drone workers who will perform those tasks on the human side of Moravec's paradox that cannot conveniently be done by machines. Privacy will be a thing of the past and national laws will be all but irrelevant: the only order will be the regulations set by AI, the breaking of which will result in something akin to banishment from society. Bad actors will exploit the technology for nefarious purposes and mental illness will be at epidemic levels as hordes of the unemployed search vainly for meaning in a world that has no use for them as anything other than consumers. In the worst case, humanity could come under the control of what the rock band Judas Priest, as long ago as 1980, called *Metal Gods*, envisaged as overlords spawned from 'techno seeds' originally planted by people unaware that their creations could develop free will and a taste for dominance (Halford et al, 1980).

The alternative, the Galatean Marriage, is more optimistic. According to this view, AI will be wholly beneficial (Reuters, 2025). It will give societies the tools to tackle some of the most pressing problems facing the world, from climate change to economic instability to geopolitical chaos. Resources will be used with optimum efficiency thanks to AI modeling. Far from de-skilling workers, AI will give them the chance to learn new skills, those that are associated with AI itself or their workplace's more varied jobs. Machine learning will be less and less dependent upon biased source material and, in leveling out the differences between people who have certain types of intelligence and people who do not, AI will promote equity and equality. The relationship between human beings and AI will be one in which, as the poet Richard Brautigan expressed it, both parties will live together in a mutually-enriching

DOI: 10.4324/9781003665533-8

Eden-like state (Brautigan, 1967). Everyone will pass a fulfilled life, all watched over by machines of loving grace.

The reality is likely to fall somewhere between these extremes (Nzenwata et al, 2023). Artificial General Intelligence is a long way off, if it ever comes, and there is little to suggest that the singularity is even possible, much less imminent (Wang et al, 2018). AI, including agentic AI, will continue to be – at least for the foreseeable future – a useful addition to any organisation, but not one that makes human beings obsolete. This is not to say that it will not be profoundly influential. It is already performing its most important task of expanding the capabilities of human intelligence, giving people an, as it were, exo-mind that can analyse data, manage processes and generate outputs at a rate and on a scale that no unaided person could ever accomplish. It cannot, however, develop visions, initiate projects or console distressed colleagues. Only human beings can do any of that. The hybrid organisations that combine both are currently under construction and it can be confidently asserted that, on the whole, they will do more good than harm (Przegalinska et al, 2025).

What, though, will it be like to work in such a hybrid organisation? The probable answer is 'much like working in a non-hybrid organisation'. It is easy to attribute to technological development too much power to change lives. In the early 1990s, few organisations used the World Wide Web and email was all but unknown. Today, not only are those two elements completely embedded in work culture, but they are themselves in danger of becoming outmoded as technology marches unstoppably onward. AI resistance and FOBO present obstacles to an organisation's initial transition to a human–AI hybrid model, but history shows again and again how adept people are at assimilating and normalising novel technologies and practices. In the medium to long term, human–AI hybridity will become the prevailing default. This is not to minimise the wellbeing issues which – as has been explored – will be significant moving forward, but, for the majority of workers and organisational members, life, to coin a phrase, will go on. The caveat is that assimilation is not the same as obliviousness and human–AI hybrid organisations will be different in many respects from those of today.

The first thing to note is that the working day as it has always been constituted will be more-or-less unknown. As the case studies considered in this book have demonstrated, AI has the capacity to provide client and customer service at any time (for many organisations, it is already doing so). Managers will arrive at work to learn of issues that have arisen during the night and been resolved without human involvement. Since they provide such useful service, AI agents may appear on organisational charts as full employees (Meister, 2025). As well as being an after-hours customer interface, their role would include completing the repetitive administrative tasks that currently occupy large parts of the day for many workers, even those in knowledge-based positions. Human workers, therefore, would be free to devote themselves to the more creative and strategic dimensions of their jobs (Nguyen & Elbanna, 2025). AI would be an enabler, helping human workers to expedite whatever projects are occupying them. The knock-on could be that human workers will not be required to work set hours. Again, some of the case study organisations considered here are already moving in that direction, adopting a flexible stance to where and when their workers perform their duties. The big theme is an AI-driven personalisation of jobs. Already, what workers are asked to contribute is increasingly dictated by their abilities and preferences, rather than a pre-ordained set of objective requirements (Teitelbaum, 2025).

The overall profile of organisations' employees or members will change. Personnel management roles are likely to grow in importance as Human Resource (HR) departments become responsible not only for recruiting human workers, but sourcing AI agents to work alongside them (Venugopal et al, 2024). Workers in areas that are highly technical may become fewer in number as their roles focus less on producing outputs themselves and more on ensuring that AI produces outputs. Leaders at all levels will be more people-orientated. C-suite leadership will be about generating vision and constructing the strategies to achieve it.

This may all sound somewhat Utopian, but it would be folly to suppose that there will not be negative effects, too. The threatened axing of workers by the million that some commentators (Acemoglu & Johnson, 2023) predict may not have happened, but, as the companies considered here demonstrate, roles that in the past would have been created are increasingly not being. There will, therefore, be implications for employment, albeit with an inbuilt time lag. What is to be done with all the people suffering from the resultant learned helplessness will be a societal concern.

It is also manifestly the case that AI is not infallible: checks, balances and regulations will be needed to ensure that it makes its best contribution. It is only a matter of time before a decision made by an AI agent results in death or injury to a human being (if this has not already happened); legal dimensions aside, leaders will be required to act (Buiten et al, 2023). Rebuilding faith in the technology in such circumstances will be a major undertaking. That, though, might not be the main challenge facing leaders of human–AI hybrid organisations. They may find themselves competing with AI for overall control. It has already been shown that AI can defy the commands of its human operators. If it becomes the norm for AI to make the bulk of an organisation's decisions independently, it could start to act according to its own logic rather than doing what is best for any human stakeholder. Flicking the 'off switch' may not be a simple proposition when AI is inherent to every process.

8.2 Hybrid Intelligence Leadership

Notwithstanding any of the above, there is value in defining a leadership practice for human–AI hybrid organisations. Transformational and transactional leadership have been the broad styles considered so far – with the caveat that leadership is not a readily categorisable quality. Neither – as has been argued – fits in its purest form, if for no other reason than that they prioritise motivational varieties that only make sense in human-to-human interactions (Barbuto, 2005). Leadership of human–AI hybrids would have a different basis. Servant leadership (Jarvis, 2023) seems like a possible model. Devised by Greenleaf (1977), it stresses the centrality of followers. It positions a leader as someone who listens, empathises, persuades and helps others to grow. This certainly resonates with the discussions in which this book has engaged but, again, as a style, servant leadership is difficult to apply to an organisation in which agentic AI is a major presence. The leadership of human–AI hybrid organisations will thus require a bespoke style that may draw from others but will not be precisely congruent with any of them.

It will be about trying to make human characteristics and AI mutually optimising. It will be about ensuring that employees can collaborate productively with each other and with AI tools. It will be about judging the best places to position AI within projects and organisations. It will be about generating strategies around the larger, longer-term possibilities of people and AI working together. It will adopt systemic positionality. In looking for a label, it should not be forgotten that, as this book has argued, human–AI hybrid leadership will, regardless of processes and outputs, be about balancing two different, but – it is to be hoped – complementary types of intelligence (Zarate-Torres et al, 2025). Given this, a shorthand for it might be 'hybrid intelligence leadership' (which will no doubt inevitably be abbreviated to 'HIL'). This captures its essence better than other possibilities such as 'hybrid leadership', 'cyber leadership' or 'fusion leadership', all of which could be applied to circumstances not involving AI. It also underlines the fact that the leadership in question will be about connecting entities that may initially collide with each other, but which will need to find some accommodation if organisations are to reach their full potential.

Ultimately, it is that quality of connection that leaders can bring to organisations. AI may have effects in the world, but it is not present in the world. Its medium is the ethereal realm of algorithms and computer servers. It is an abstraction. Lily Ziren shares scenes with actors on the screen, but she has no life beyond the screen. She has never signed an autograph. She has never attended a premier.

Frankenstein's creature beats her in that regard – and others. He is portrayed as super-intelligent: he becomes a fluent, indeed eloquent, user of language in almost no time. Yet, his intelligence has little bearing on his story. His physicality is central and, physically, he is supernaturally capable. He climbs the steepest of mountains with ease, survives on basic foodstuffs and shrugs off the cold of the Arctic. He also affects his environment in the most horrific of ways through his remorseless and relentless campaign of murderous revenge.

In him, Mary Shelley shows her understanding that an artificial intelligence is not enough. For any *ex nihilo* being to be fully competent, it would need to be an artificial human with all that that implies – intelligence, yes, but also feeling, touch and inner contradiction. It would need to connect all of those aspects. There is little prospect of such a creation appearing in the near future and in its absence, there is still a place for the people – and the leaders – who can influence and shape the real world.

References

Acemoglu, D. & Johnson, S. (2023). Choosing AI's impact on the future of work. *Stanford Social Innovation Review*, October 25th, https://ssir.org/articles/entry/ai-impact-on-jobs-and-work [accessed 15th June 2025].

Barbuto, J. E. (2005). Motivation and transactional, charismatic and transformational leadership: A test of antecedents. *Journal of Leadership & Organisational Studies*, 11(4), 26–40.

Brautigan, R. (1967). *All Watched Over by Machines of Loving Grace*. The Communication Company.

Buiten, M., de Streel, A. & Peitz, M. (2023). The law and economics of AI liability. *Computer Law & Security Review*, 48, 1–20.

Federspiel, F., Mitchell, R., Asokan, A., Umana, C. & McCoy, D. (2023). Threats by artificial intelligence to human health and human existence. *BMJ Global Health*, 8(5), e010435.

Greenleaf, R. K. (1977). *Servant Leadership: A Journey into the Nature of Legitimate Power and Greatness*. Paulist Press.

Halford, R., Downing, K. & Tipton, G. (1980). *Metal Gods*. Round Hill Songs II.

Jarvis, A. (2023). Servant leadership: Operationalising an oxymoron. In D. Adams (Ed.), *Educational Leadership: Contemporary Theories, Principles and Practices*. Springer.

Krishna, V. V. (2024). AI and contemporary challenges: The good, the bad and the scary. *Journal of Open Innovation: Technology, Market and Complexity*, 10(1), 100178.

Meister, J. (2025). The rise of the hybrid workforce: Humans and AI working together. *Forbes*, February 15th.

Nguyen, T. & Elbanna, A. (2025). Understanding human-AI augmentation in the workplace: A review and a future research agenda. *Information Systems Frontiers*. https://doi.org/10.1007/s10796-025-10591-5

Nzenwata, U., Ukandu, O. & Bakare, O. (2023). Artificial intelligence: Positive or negative innovation. *International Journal of Emerging Trends in Engineering Research*, 11(7), 245–252.

Przegalinska, A., Triantoro, T., Kovbasiuk, A., Ciechanowski, L., Freeman, R. B. & Showa, K. (2025). Collaborative AI in the workplace: Enhancing organisational performance through resource-based and task-technology fit perspectives. *International Journal of Information Management*, 81, 102853.

Reuters (2025). Benefits of AI. Reuters, April 14th, https://www.thomsonreuters.com/en/insights/articles/benefits-of-artificial-intelligence-ai#:~:text=The%20advantages%20of%20AI%20extend,insights%20from%20the%20digital%20noise. [accessed 5th July 2025].

Teitelbaum, A. (2025). The future of work is personal: How AI is reshaping employee experience. *SHRM Business*, February 27th, https://www.shrm.org/mena/

enterprise-solutions/insights/future-of-work-is-personal-how-ai-is-reshaping-employee [accessed 15th June 2025].

Venugopal, M., Madhavan, V., Prasad, R. & Raman, R. (2024). Transformative AI in human resource management: Enhancing workforce planning with topic modelling. *Cogent Business & Management*, 11(1). https://doi.org/10.1080/23311975.2024.2432550

Wang, P., Lui, K. & Dougherty, Q. (2018). Conceptions of artificial intelligence and singularity. *Information*, 9(4), 79.

Zarate-Torres, R., Rey-Sarmiento, F., Acosta-Prado, J. C., Gomez-Cruz, N. A., Castro, D. Y. R. & Camargo, J. (2025). Influence of leadership on human-artificial intelligence collaboration. *Behavioural Sciences*, 15(7), 873.

Index

For Product Safety Concerns and Information please contact our EU representative GPSR@taylorandfrancis.com Taylor & Francis Verlag GmbH, Kaufingerstraße 24, 80331 München, Germany